Stitch by Stitch

Volume 14

TORSTAR BOOKS

NEW YORK · TORONTO

Stitch by Stitch

TORSTAR BOOKS INC.
300 E.42ND STREET
NEW YORK, NY 10017

Knitting and crochet abbreviations

approx = approximately
beg = begin(ning)
ch = chain(s)
cm = centimeter(s)
cont = continue(ing)
dc = double crochet
dec = decreas(e)(ing)
dtr = double triple
foll = follow(ing)
g = gram(s)
grp = group(s)
dc = half double
  crochet

in = inch(es)
inc = increase(e)(ing)
K = knit
oz = ounce(s)
P = purl
patt = pattern
psso = pass slipped
  stitch over
rem = remain(ing)
rep = repeat
RS = right side
sc = single crochet
sl = slip

sl st = slip stitch
sp = space(s)
st(s) = stitch(es)
tbl = through back of
  loop(s)
tog = together
tr = triple crochet
WS = wrong side
wyib = with yarn in
  back
wyif = with yarn in front
yd = yard(s)
yo = yarn over

A guide to the pattern sizes

		10	12	14	16	18	20
Bust	in	32½	34	36	38	40	42
	cm	83	87	92	97	102	107
Waist	in	25	26½	28	30	32	34
	cm	64	67	71	76	81	87
Hips	in	34½	36	38	40	42	44
	cm	88	92	97	102	107	112

Torstar Books also offers a range of acrylic book stands, designed to keep instructional books such as *Stitch by Stitch* open, flat and upright while leaving the hands free for practical work.

For information write to Torstar Books Inc., 300 E.42nd Street, New York, NY 10017.

Library of Congress Cataloging in Publication Data
Main entry under title:

Stitch by stitch.

Includes index.
1. Needlework. I. Torstar Books (Firm)
TT705.S74 1984   746.4   84-111
ISBN 0-920269-00-1 (set)

98765432

© Marshall Cavendish Limited 1984

Printed in Belgium

ISBN 0-920269-14-1 (Volume 14)

Step-by-Step Crochet Course

Step-by-Step Knitting Course

Step-by-Step Sewing Course

Step-by-Step Needlework Course

Extra Special Crochet

Extra Special Knitting

Extra Special Sewing

Homemaker

Shoestring

Crochet / COURSE 61

Different methods of shaping

You have already learned how to shape a horizontally-worked crochet fabric by increasing or decreasing stitches at the side of the fabric or in the middle. In this course we show you two more ways to produce a shaped fabric.

Both methods involve a fabric in which the rows run vertically. The first method exploits the different depths of the basic crochet stitches: by changing to progressively deeper stitches as you work down the fabric and shallower ones as you work up, you produce a flared fabric. This method is often used in shaping a skirt or a long sleeve.

In the other method—sometimes called "short-row" shaping—certain rows are left unworked at one end of the fabric. By working a few more stitches each time on subsequent alternate rows until all the stitches have once more been worked along the length of the fabric, you achieve a curved shape in the fabric. The method is ideal for shaping a beret.

Shaping with different stitches

Use this method when working a flared or fluted fabric. The shallow single crochet stitches should be used to form the narrowest section, such as a neck or waist edge, followed by half doubles for a wider section—the hipline of a skirt or the bodice of a fitted jacket, for example—and double crochet stitches for the widest part of the garment.

The crochet is worked from the side edge to the side edge, so that the stitches lie horizontally across the fabric. This should be taken into account when planning a design in which only one part is to be shaped in this way, since it is important to make sure that stitches which lie horizontally across the fabric blend in with those worked vertically. Decide where shaping falls on the garment so the stitches occur in the right place.

1 Make a length of chain equal to the length required for the side edge, with one extra turning chain. Work the first section (top of a skirt or sleeve) in single crochet. Mark the last single crochet with a contrasting-colored thread.

2 Now crochet the next section in half doubles. Mark the last stitch with a colored thread in the same way as before, so that you can see exactly where each section begins and ends. Our sample contains 10 single crochets and 10 half double stitches.

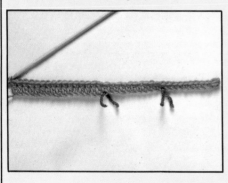

3 Now continue in double crochet to the end of the chain. These double stitches form the widest part of the crochet fabric and should be used for the wide edge of the garment.

4 Continue to crochet the different stitches in the correct positions, so that the next row will begin with 3 chains followed by a double worked into each double, a half double into each half double and a single crochet into each single crochet, completing the row by working the last stitch into the turning chain.

5 Continue to keep the stitches in the correct sections on every row until the fabric is the desired width. When making a skirt, measure the width of the single crochet section, making sure that it is equivalent to half the waist measurement. Our finished sample shows the A-line effect achieved in this way.

"Short-row" shaping

In this method the fabric is worked from side edge to side edge in the same way as in the previous method, but stitches are left unworked at the end of a row until a later stage to achieve the curved effect. Our step-by-step pictures are intended only as a guide, to help you when shaping a garment in this way, since the number of stitches left unworked at the end of the row will vary, depending on how sharply the shaping line needs to curve in the center of the fabric. Stitches that are shaped in groups of ten will curve more sharply than those worked in groups of five, for example, and this should be taken into account when you are planning to shape a garment in this way.

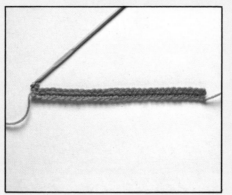

1 Make the number of chains required for the side edge of the fabric and work two single crochet rows on these stitches.
To make our sample begin with 31 chains, then work 30 single crochets in each row.

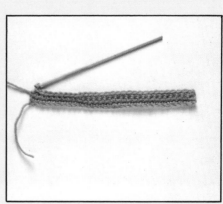

2 Now work 20 single crochets in the next row, then slip stitch across the last 10 stitches. By slip stitching across the stitches, rather than turning and leaving the stitches unworked at this point, you achieve a more gentle shaping in the center of the fabric.

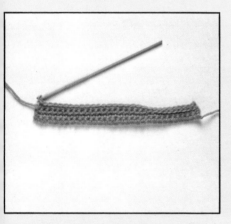

3 Turn and work one slip stitch into each of the next 10 slip stitches, then work a single crochet into each single crochet to the end of the row, including the turning chain.

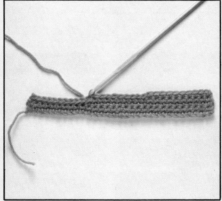

4 Turn. Make 1 chain, then work a single crochet into each of the next 10 stitches. Slip stitch into each of the next 10 single crochets.

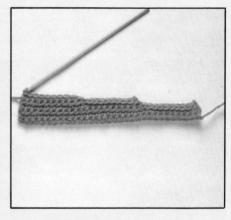

5 Turn and repeat step 3 once more so that only 10 single crochets have been worked in the last two rows. This completes one side of the shaping.

6 Now begin to shape the other side of the curve. Work 1 single crochet into each of the first 10 single crochets then into each of the next 10 slip stitches.

7 Turn, leaving the remaining stitches at the left-hand side unworked, and work 1 single crochet into each of the stitches worked in the previous row.

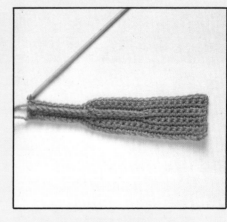

8 Continue to shape the 2nd side of the curve by working a single crochet into each of the stitches worked in the previous row and into the remaining slip stitches to the side edge.

continued

Fred Mancini

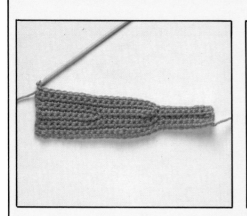

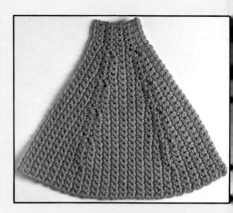

9 Turn and crochet back to the side edge in single crochet as before to complete the shaping curve.

10 This sample shows several blocks of stitches shaped in this way with two straight rows of single crochet between each shaped section. This forms a curved fabric suitable for a hat or beret, which can be made by sewing the side edges together once the crochet is the required size and then gathering the top edge to form the crown of the hat.

11 A flatter shaping has been achieved in this sample by working in exactly the same way as before, but working five stitches less each time on the first side of the curve, then five stitches more on the 2nd side of the curve.

Stitch Wise

Close shell pattern

Make a number of chains divisible by 5 plus 1.
Base row 2dc into 4th ch from hook, 1ch, 2dc into next ch, *skip 3ch, 2dc into next ch, 1ch, 2dc into next ch, rep from * to end, ending with 1dc into last ch. Turn.
1st row 3ch, work (2dc, 1ch, 2dc—called 1 shell—) into each 1ch sp, ending with 1dc into top of turning ch. Turn.
2nd row 3ch, work 1 shell into first 1ch sp, 2ch, insert hook from front to back into 1ch sp at center of first shell in previous row and work 1sc into this sp—called 1sc below—, *2ch, 1 shell into next 1ch sp, 2ch, 1sc below into next 1ch sp at center of next shell in previous row, rep from * ending with 1 shell into last 1ch sp, 1dc into top of turning ch. Turn.
3rd row 3ch, *1 shell into next 1ch sp, rep from * to end, ending with 1dc into top of turning ch. Turn.
2nd and 3rd rows form pattern and are repeated throughout.

Crossed shell pattern

Make a number of chains divisible by 6.
Base row 1hdc into 3rd ch from hook, 1hdc into each ch to end. Turn.
1st row 2ch, skip first hdc, 3hdc into next hdc—called 1 shell—, *skip 2hdc, 1 shell into next hdc, rep from * to end, 1hdc into top of turning ch. Turn.
2nd row 3ch, 1dc into 3rd hdc of first shell, 1ch, 1dc into *first* dc of first shell crossing 2nd dc over first at front—called CrdcF—, *1dc into 3rd dc of next shell, 1ch, CrdcF into first dc of same shell, rep from * to end, 1dc into top of turning ch. Turn.
3rd row 2ch, 1 shell into 1 ch sp at center of first crossed dc group, *1 shell into 1ch sp at center of next crossed dc group, rep from * to end. 1hdc into top of ch. Turn. 2nd and 3rd rows form pattern and are repeated throughout.

Flared skirt and bolero

A pretty outfit to suit any girl. It has a neatly shaped skirt and matching bolero, onto which is sewn a flower motif.

Sizes
Skirt To fit 28[30:32]in (71[76:81]cm) hips.
Length, 16½[19:21¼]in (42[48:53]cm).
Bolero To fit 26[28:30]in (66[71:76]cm) chest.
Length, 13[14½:16½]in (33[36.5:42]cm).
Note: Directions for larger sizes are in brackets []; if there is only one set of figures it applies to all sizes.

Materials
Skirt and bolero 11[12:13]oz (280[300:320]g) of a sport yarn in main shade (A)
1[1:2]oz (20[20:40]g) in contrasting color (B)
Sizes C and E (3.00 and 3.50mm) crochet hooks
Waist length (plus seam allowance) of 1in (2.5in)-wide elastic

Gauge
21dc and 12 rows to 4in (10cm) worked on size E (3.50mm) hook.

Skirt (worked in one piece)

Using size E (3.50mm) hook and A, make 87[101:113]ch.
Base row 1dc into 3rd ch from hook, 1dc into each of next 54[62:68]ch, 1hdc into

Stuart Macleod

7

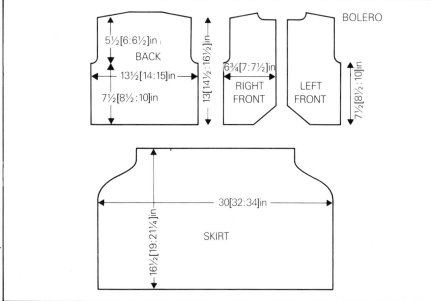

each of next 20[26:32]ch, 1sc into each of last 10sc. Turn. 86[100:112] sts.

1st row 1ch, skip first sc, 1sc into each sc, 1hdc into each hdc and 1dc into each dc worked in previous row, 1dc into top of turning ch. Turn.

2nd row 3ch, skip first dc, 1dc into each dc, 1hdc into each hdc and 1sc into each sc worked in previous row, 1sc into top of turning ch. Turn.

Keeping stitches in correct sequence, rep last 2 rows until hdc section measures 30[32:34]in (76[81:86]cm) for hip measurement. Fasten off.

Lower border
Using size C (3.00mm) hook, A and with RS facing, rejoin yarn to corner of lower (dc) edge.

1st row 1ch, *1sc into next row end, 2sc into next row end, rep from * to end, changing to B on last st. Turn.

2nd row Using B, 1ch, skip first st, 1sc into each sc to end. Turn.
Rep 2nd row twice more. Fasten off.

To finish
Press or block according to yarn used. Join back seam of skirt. Join waist length of elastic into circle. Work a herringbone casing over elastic at WS of waist. Press seam.

Bolero

Back
Using size E (3.50mm) hook and A, make 75[79:85]ch.

Base row 1hdc into 3rd ch from hook, 1hdc into each ch to end. 74[78:84] sts.

Patt row 2ch, skip first hdc, 1hdc into each hdc to end, 1hdc into top of turning ch. Turn.
Rep patt row until back measures 7½[8½:10]in (19[21.5:25.5]cm).

Shape armholes
1st row Sl st across first 4 sts, 2ch, 1hdc into each st to last 3 sts, turn.

68[72:78] sts.

2nd row 2ch, skip first hdc, 1hdc into next hdc, leaving last loop of each on hook work 1hdc into each of next 2hdc, yo and draw through all loops on hook—called decrease 1 or dec 1—, 1hdc into each hdc to last 4 sts, dec 1, 1hdc into each of last 2 sts. Turn.
Rep 2nd row once more. 64[68:74] sts.
Cont straight until armhole measures 5½[6:6½]in (14[15:16.5]cm); end with a RS row.

Shape shoulders
1st row Sl st across first 5 sts, 2ch, 1hdc into each of next 11[12:14] sts, turn and complete first shoulder on these sts.
Next row Patt to within last 4[4:5] sts, turn.
Next row Sl st across first 5[5:6] sts, 2ch, 1hdc into each st to end. Fasten off.
With WS of work facing return to rem sts, skip next 32[34:36] sts, rejoin yarn to next st, 2ch, patt to within last 4 sts, turn.
Next row Sl st across first 5 sts, patt to end. Turn.
Next row Patt to within last 4[4:5] sts. Fasten off.

Right front
Using size E (3.50mm) hook and A, make 22[24:27]ch.
Base row 1hdc into 3rd ch from hook, 1hdc into each ch to end. Turn. 21[23:26]hdc.

Shape front edge
1st row 5ch, 1hdc into 3rd ch from hook, 1hdc into each of next 2ch, 1hdc into each st to end. Turn. 25[27:30] sts.
2nd row 2ch, skip first hdc, 1hdc into each st to end. 1hdc into top of turning ch. Turn. Rep last 2 rows 3 times more. 37[39:42] sts. Cont straight until front measures same as back to armholes; end at side edge.

Shape armhole
1st row Sl st across first 4 sts, 2ch, 1hdc into each st to end. Turn.

2nd row Patt to within last 4 sts, dec 1, patt to end. Turn.

3rd row 2ch, skip first hdc, 1hdc into next hdc, dec 1, patt to end. Turn. 32[34:37] sts. Cont in patt straight until armhole measures 3 rows less than back armhole; end at armhole edge.

Shape neck
Next row Patt to within last 14[15:16] sts, turn.
Dec one st at neck edge on next 2 rows.

Shape shoulder
1st row Patt to within last 4 sts, turn.
2nd row Sl st across first 5[5:6] sts, 2ch, patt to end. Turn.
3rd row Patt to within last 4[4:5] sts. Fasten off.

Left front
Work as for right front, reversing armhole and shoulder shaping.

To finish
Press or block as for skirt. Join seams.

The border
Using size C (3.00mm) hook, A and with RS facing, rejoin yarn to center ch at lower edge of back. Work 1sc into each ch along back and front edges, then up lower front shaping, working 1sc into each st and row end, work (1sc into next row end, 2sc into next row end) up straight section of front edge to neck, 3sc into corner, then 1sc into each st along neck edge. Work down other side to center back in same way, joining in B to last st. Turn.
Next row Using B, 1ch, 1sc into each sc all around. Turn.
Rep last row twice more. Fasten off. Join small seam of border.

Armhole borders (alike)
With A, work a row of sc evenly around armhole, then work 1 row in B. Fasten off.

Flower motif
Using size C (3.00mm) hook and A, make 6ch, join with sl st to first ch.
1st round 1ch to count as first sc, 15sc into circle. Join with sl st to first ch.
2nd round 6ch, skip first sc,* 1dc into next sc, 3ch, skip next sc, rep from * 6 times more. Join with sl st to 3rd of first 6ch. (Eight 3-ch spaces.) Cut off A.
3rd round Join B to first sp worked in previous round, work (1sc, 1hdc, 3dc, 1hdc, 1sc) into each 3-ch sp. Join with sl st to first sc. Fasten off. Sew motif to front.

Ties (Make 2)
Using size C (3.00mm) hook and 2 strands of B, make 100ch.
Next row (make bobble) Sl st into 4th ch from hook, so making small loop on end of ch, 3ch, 12dc into this small loop. Fasten off. Darn in end.
Using spare length of yarn at other end of ch, attach tie to neck of bolero.

Brian Mayor

Crochet with sequins

Sequins can be threaded onto crochet yarn and used to make beautiful fabrics in the same way as when combining beads with crochet (see Volume 12, page 10). Because sequins are much lighter than beads, they can be worked all over your crochet fabric and used effectively to make heavily encrusted sequin patterns. Different colored sequins worked in stripes on a chevron crochet pattern make an ideal fabric for a vest or jacket, while a fine lace pattern scattered with sequins would make a perfect evening top or shawl.

Sequins are available in a variety of sizes, ranging from the smallest, measuring about $\frac{1}{4}$in (6mm) to a large $\frac{7}{8}$in (22mm) sequin which is best used with a double fabric.

The best results are obtained by introducing the sequin while working a wrong-side row so that the sequin is held firmly in place on the right side of the work. A sequin worked on the right side is held more loosely, creating an untidy patterned fabric.

1 Sequins to be used with crochet can be of any size but must have a hole at the **edge** rather than at the center to ensure that they hang evenly on the crochet fabric.

2 If the hole is large enough, thread the sequins directly onto the yarn using a fine needle. For a smaller hole or if the yarn is too thick, use the cotton loop method described in Volume 10, page 52 to thread the sequins onto the yarn.

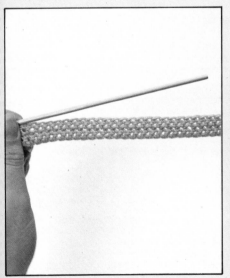

3 Your instructions will usually tell you how many sequins should be threaded onto each ball of yarn for your pattern. For a single crochet fabric work two or three rows before introducing the sequins.

4 Sequin row: one chain, skip first stitch, one single crochet into next stitch. Insert the hook into the next stitch and draw through a loop.

5 Push the sequin up close to the work so that it lies flat against the fabric. Hold the sequin with the index finger of the left hand if necessary to ensure that it remains flat while working the stitch.

continued

Mike Berend

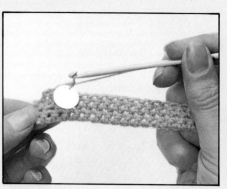

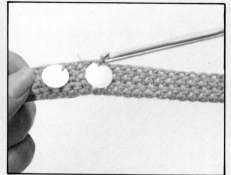

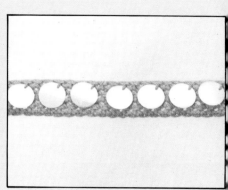

6 Here we show you the right side of the crochet fabric with the sequin held firmly in place at the top.

7 Work 2 single crochets, then work another sequin into the next stitch so that they lie side by side on the right side of the work as shown here.

8 Continue to work a sequin stitch on every third stitch across the row, with a single crochet only into the top of the turning chain at the edge of the fabric.

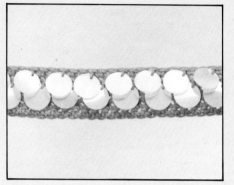

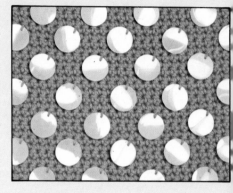

9 Work one single crochet row on the right side of the fabric, then change the position of the sequins on the following row, so that they lie between the sequins worked previously, by working the first sequin into the 2nd stitch.

10 By alternating the sequin rows with a single crochet row you will obtain a solid sequin fabric as shown here.

11 This picture shows sequins worked in a scattered pattern on a single crochet fabric.

Working half doubles with sequins

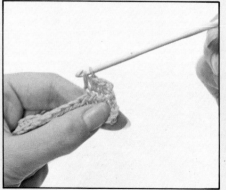

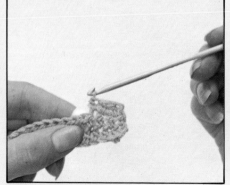

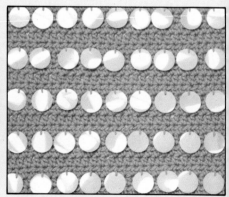

1 Attach the sequins from the wrong side of the fabric for the best results. Crochet two or three half double rows before beginning sequin pattern. Work to position for first sequin. Wind yarn over the hook, insert the hook into the next stitch and draw through a loop so that there are 3 loops on the hook.

2 Slip the sequin up to the hook on the wrong side. Wind the yarn over the hook at the far side of the sequin, holding the sequin flat against the fabric and complete the half double in the normal way.

3 Here we show you the right side of the half double fabric with sequins worked on every 3rd row for a scattered effect.

Working doubles with sequins

The best results are obtained by introducing the sequins on the wrong side of a double fabric in the same way as when working a single crochet or half double pattern. Sequins introduced on the right side of the work cannot be looped so firmly into position, so they are likely to twist rather than hang evenly across the fabric. Use larger sequins to cover a double fabric and smaller sequins when working a scattered pattern.

1 Work to the position for the first sequin. Wind yarn over hook, insert hook into next stitch, wind yarn over hook, draw through a loop then wind yarn over hook and draw through 2 loops to complete the first stage.

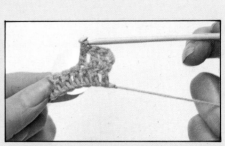

2 Push the sequin up close to the hook making sure that it lies absolutely flat against the right side of the work, holding the sequin with the left hand if necessary. Complete the double in the normal way.

3 Here we show you the right side of the work. The sequin is held firmly in place at the top of the double just worked.

4 This completed sample shows large sequins worked on every wrong side row so that double fabric has been completely covered by the sequins.

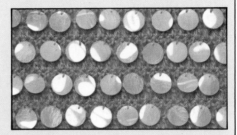

5 Here smaller sequins have been combined with mohair on every other row, alternating the position so that the sequin lies at the center of the sequins worked in the previous row.

Mike Berend

Stitch Wise

Sequin shell pattern

Make a number of chains divisible by 10 plus 1 with 2 extra turning chains.

1st row (RS) 1dc into 4th ch from hook, *3ch, skip 3ch, work (2dc, 2ch, 2dc) into next ch, 3ch, skip 3ch, 1dc into each of next 3ch, rep from * to end, ending last rep with 1dc into each of last 2ch. Turn.

2nd row 3ch to count as first dc, yo, insert hook into next dc, yo and draw through a loop, yo and draw through 2 loops on hook, sl sequin up to hook, yo at far side of sequin and draw yarn through 2 loops on hook—called S1dc—, *3ch, (2dc, 2ch, 2dc) into next 2ch sp, 3ch, 1dc into next dc, S1dc into next dc, 1dc into next dc, rep from * to end, working last dc into top of turning ch. Turn.

3rd row 3ch to count as first dc, 1dc into next dc, *3ch to count as first dc, 1dc into next dc, *3ch, (2dc, 2ch, 2dc) into next 2ch sp, 3ch, 1dc into each of next 3dc, rep from * to end, ending last rep with 3ch, 1dc into next dc, 1dc into top of turning ch. Turn.

2nd and 3rd rows form patt and are rep throughout.

Diagonal sequin pattern

Make a number of chains divisible by 6 plus 1.

Base row 1sc into 3rd ch from hook, 1sc into each ch to end. Turn.

1st row (WS) 1ch, skip first st, 1sc into next st, *insert hook into next sc, yo and draw through a loop, sl sequin up to hook, yo at far side of sequin and draw loop through 2 loops on hook—called S1sc—, 1sc into each of next 5sc, rep from * to last 5 sts, S1sc, 1sc into each of next 3 sts, 1sc into turning ch. Turn.

2nd and every alternate row 1ch, skip first st, 1sc int each sc and S1sc to end, 1sc into turning ch. Turn.

3rd row 1ch, skip first st, 1sc into next sc,*S1sc, 1sc into each of next 5sc, rep from * to end, working last sc into turning ch. Turn.

5th row 1ch, skip first st, *1sc into each of next 5 sts, S1sc, rep from * to end, S1sc into turning ch. Turn.

7th row 1ch, skip first st, 1sc into each of next 4 sts, *S1sc, 1sc into each of next 5 sts, rep from * to last 5 sts. S1sc into next st, 1sc into each of next 3 sts, 1sc into turning ch. Turn.

9th row 1ch, skip first st, 1sc into each of next 3 sts, *S1sc, 1sc into each of next 5 sts, rep from * to last 3 sts, S1sc, 1sc into next st, 1sc into turning ch. Turn.

11th row 1ch, skip first st, 1sc into each of next 2 sts, *S1sc, 1sc into each of next 5 sts, rep from * to last 4 sts, S1sc, 1sc into each st to end, 1sc into turning ch. Turn.

12th row As 2nd.

3rd to 12th rows form patt and are rep throughout.

Sequined evening top and cardigan

Ross Greetham

For that special evening out: a dazzling top and cardigan.

Sizes To fit 32[34:36]in (81[86:91]cm) bust.
Length, 15in (38cm) excluding straps.
Cardigan To fit 32[34:36]in (81[86:91]cm) bust.
Length, 22[22½:23]in (58[59:60]cm).
Sleeve seam, 15¾in (40cm).
Note: Directions for larger sizes are in brackets []; if there is only one set of figures it applies to all sizes.

Materials
Sport yarn
Top 9[10:11]oz (225[250:275]g)
Approx. 3000×⅝in (1.5cm) sequins
Size C (3.00mm) crochet hook
7in (18cm) zipper
Cardigan 22[23:24]oz (600[625:650]g)
Approx. 300×⅝in (1.5cm) sequins
Size C (3.00mm) crochet hook

Gauge
24 sts and 20 rows to 4in (10cm) worked on size C (3.00mm) hook.

Evening top

Note: Thread approx. 300 sequins onto each ball of yarn.

Back
Using size C (3.00mm) hook make 102[108:114]ch.

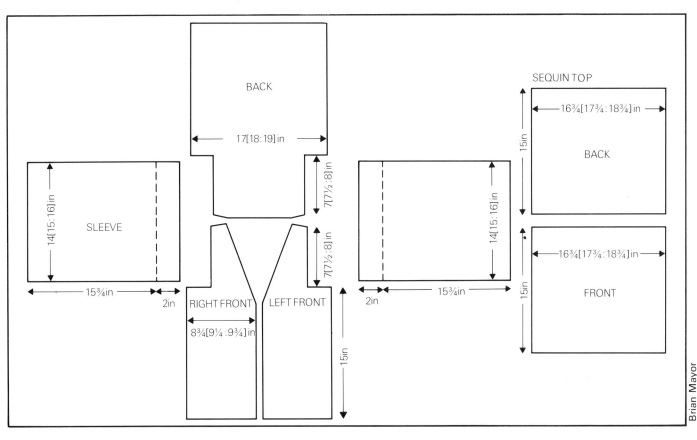

Brian Mayor

Base row 1hdc into 3rd ch from hook, 1hdc into each ch to end. Turn.
Beg patt
1st row (WS) 2ch, *yo and insert hook into next st, yo and draw loop through, push sequin up close to hook, yo at far side of sequin and draw through all loops on hook–1hdc sequin or 1hdcS–, 1hdc into each of next 2hdc, rep from * to end, working last hdc into top of turning ch. Turn.
2nd row 2ch, skip first st, 1hdc into each st to end, 1hdc into top of turning ch. Turn. These 2 rows form patt. Cont in patt until work measures 15in (38cm); end with a 1st row. Do not turn but work a row of crab st (sc worked from left to right). Fasten off.

Front
Work as given for back.

Straps (make 2)
Using yarn double throughout make a chain of length required for doubled shoulder strap.
Next row 1hdc into 3rd ch from hook, 1hdc into each ch to end. Fasten off.

To finish
Do not press. Join right side seam. Join left side seam, leaving 7in (18cm) open at top for zipper. Sew in zipper. Sew on straps, approx. 3in (8cm) from side seams.

Cardigan

Note: Thread approx. 10 sequins on each 1oz (25g) ball of yarn.
Back
Using size C (3.00mm) hook, make 105[111:117]ch.
Base row Work 1sc and 1dc into 5th ch from hook, *skip next ch, 1sc and 1dc into next ch, rep from * to within last 2ch, skip next ch, 1sc into last ch. Turn.
Beg patt
Patt row 3ch, *1sc and 1dc into next sc, rep from * to end, 1sc into top of turning ch. Turn. Mark this row for RS of work. This row forms patt. Cont in patt, working sequins on dc sts as required (see page 11), until work measures 15in (38cm); end with a WS row.**
Shape armholes
Next row Sl st across 12 sts and into 13th st, 3ch to count as first dc, work in patt to within last 13 sts, 1sc into next dc, turn. Cont straight until armholes measure 7[7½:8]in (18[19:20]cm); end with a WS row.
Shape shoulders
Next row Sl st across first 8 sts and into 9th st, 3ch, patt 12[14:16] sts, 1sc into next st, turn.
Next row Patt 7[8:9] sts. Fasten off. With RS of work facing skip center 33[35:37] sts and rejoin yarn to next st. Complete to match first side.

Left front
Using size C (3.00mm) hook, make 55[59:61]ch. Work as for back to **.
Shape armhole and front edge
Next row Sl st across first 12 sts and into 13th st, 3ch to count as first dc, patt to within last 3 sts, 1sc into next dc, turn. 38[42:44] sts. Patt 3 rows without shaping.
Next row Patt to within last 3 sts, 1sc into next dc, turn. 36[40:42] sts. Keeping armhole edge straight, cont in patt dec 2 sts at neck edge on every foll 4th row until 22[24:26] sts rem. Cont straight until armhole measures same as back to shoulder; end with a WS row.
Shape shoulder
Next row Sl st across first 8 sts and into 9th st, 3ch, patt to end.
Next row Patt 7[8:9] sts. Fasten off.

Right front
Work as for left front, reversing all shaping.

Sleeves
Using size C (3.00mm) hook make 89[95:101]ch. Work base row and patt row as for back. Cont in patt with scattered sequins until sleeve measures 15¾in (40cm). Mark ends of last row with colored thread. Cont in patt for 2in (5cm). Fasten off.

To finish
Do not press. Join shoulder and side seams. Set in sleeves and join sleeve seams.
For borders, with RS facing rejoin yarn to lower edge of side seam and work sc evenly around outer edge. Join with sl st to first sc. Do not turn. Work a row of crab stitch. Join with sl st to first st. Fasten off. Finish lower edge of sleeves in same way.

*Filet lace insertions
*Inserting the filet strips into fabric
*Stitch Wise: filet patterns worked from a chart
*Patterns for a tablecloth and napkins

Filet lace insertions

The technique of inserting filet lace strips into fabric just above the hemmed edge was used extensively in the 19th century to trim household items. Tablecloths, traycloths, sheets, towels and baby linen were all treated this way, trimmed either with strips of plain filet mesh or with more intricate patterns using flower or animal motifs, monograms, words and even phrases such as "Sleep, Baby, Sleep".

Today, with the imaginative use of bright-colored fabrics and matching crochet cotton, we can use this technique to enhance table linen in more modern styles.

The patterns are worked from a chart using the same method described in Volume 7, page 22. Motifs with clear outlines or simple geometric patterns produce the best results. Cross-stitch embroidery patterns, simple illustrations from books or magazines and Fair Isle and jacquard knitting patterns are all sources of inspiration.

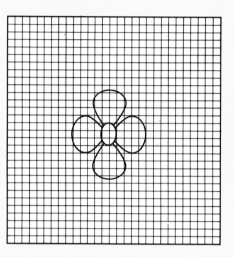

1 Most filet patterns are set out in the form of a chart (see Volume 7, page 22). To plan your own design draw your motif on graph paper, using clear outlines.

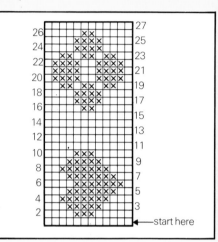

2 Translate the design into graph form using an X for each block and a blank square for each space. Motifs for an insertion to be placed around the base of the fabric will lie horizontally along the strip, although the graph should be worked vertically in the normal way as shown here.

3 The filet insertions are worked from side edge to side edge so that the first row of the pattern equals the width of the strip as shown here, although the filet strip will be worked horizontally from left to right in the normal way. The length is determined by the number of rows worked. Plan to leave at least one row of spaces at either side of the motif so that it stands out against the mesh background.

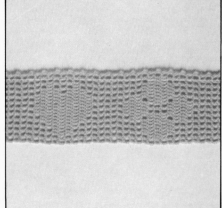

4 When working a motif pattern the best results are obtained by using a fine filet mesh (see Volume 7, page 22), where 1 double, 1 chain and 1 double form the spaces, with 3 doubles worked in each block. For consecutive blocks add 2 doubles each time.

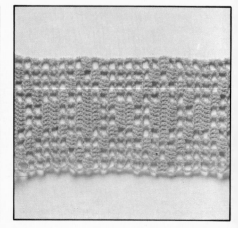

5 For a geometric pattern like the one shown here, use a more widely spaced filet mesh, in which 1 double, 2 chains and 1 double form the spaces, with 4 doubles worked in each block (see Volume 7, page 18). For consecutive blocks add 3 doubles each time.

Inserting the filet strips into fabric

Filet insertions can be used in a variety of ways as a decorative trimming for household linen. Wide strips can be inserted approximately 3in (7.5cm) from the lower edge, all the way around a circular, square or rectangular tablecloth. Long strips can be sewn across the middle of a tablecloth, dividing it into four sections, or narrow lace strips can be used to decorate a tray cloth, by inserting the filet lace into each end of the cloth in the traditional way.

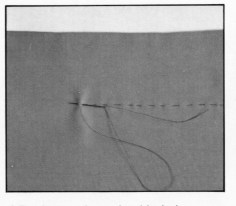

1 To trim a ready-made tablecloth, decide where you wish your insertion to come at the lower edge and sew a line of basting stitches around the cloth at this point (first marking it with tailor's chalk, if you like), making evenly spaced stitches about ⅜in (1cm) apart.

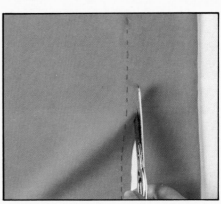

2 Cut the fabric ⅝in (1.5cm) outside this all the way around the fabric. There are now two pieces; the main center section and the narrow edge strip. Use the same method whether trimming a circular, square or long tablecloth.

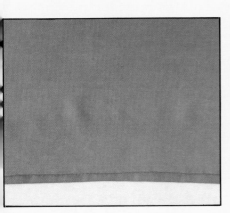

3 Turn under the edge of the center section along the line of basting stitches and pin, baste and hem it in place. Treat the raw edge of the narrow strip in the same way. Press the hems firmly.

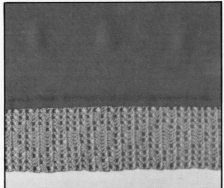

4 Press or block the filet insertion, depending on the yarn used, making sure that the mesh runs in straight lines. Lay the wrong side of the fabric on the right side of the filet insertion so that it just overlaps at the top edge, making sure the fabric lies smoothly on the crochet.

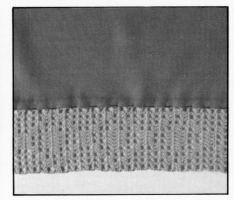

5 Baste the fabric in place as before all around the edge of the fabric, using small even stitches and a contrasting thread.

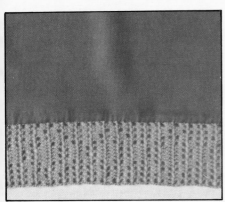

6 Now overcast the insertion firmly in place with tiny stitches and matching thread; or use machine zig-zag stitch if you prefer.

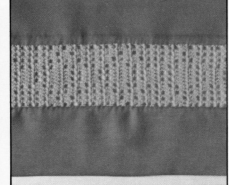

7 Now baste, then stitch, the hemmed edge of the narrow strip to the other side of the filet insertion in the same way as before, making sure that the filet strip lies absolutely flat all the way around.

8 To insert crochet in the form of a cross, first make one long strip and two short strips and sew them together in the middle as shown here.

continued

Fred Mancini

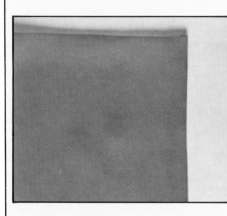

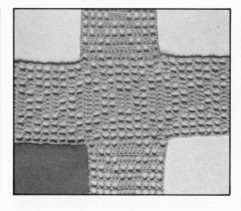

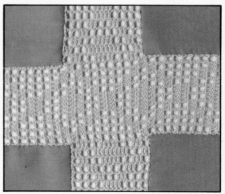

9 Cut the fabric into four equal quarters, turn the raw edges to the wrong side and hem in place as before.

10 Now lay the first quarter over the filet cross and baste, then sew, in place as before. Be careful to work the corner as neatly as possible.

11 Apply each quarter to the center filet cross insertion in the same way to complete the cloth. A circular or rectangular cloth can be treated in the same way, cutting out either four quarter circles or dividing the rectangle into four and completing the cloth as above.

Stitch Wise

Diamond pattern

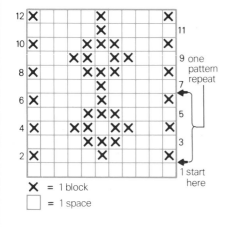

✕ = 1 block
☐ = 1 space

Make 25ch.

1st row 1dc into 6th ch from hook, *1ch, skip 1ch, 1dc into next ch, rep from * to end. Turn.
Beg with the 2nd row, cont to work in patt from chart. Even (WS) rows are worked from left to right and uneven (RS) rows from right to left.

Shamrock pattern

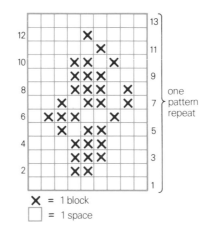

✕ = 1 block
☐ = 1 space

Make 22ch.

1st row 1dc into 6th ch from hook, * 1ch, skip 1ch, 1dc into next ch, rep from * to end. Turn.
Beginning with the 2nd row cont to work from chart. Even (WS) rows are worked from left to right and uneven (RS) rows from right to left.

Diagonal pattern

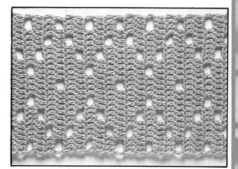

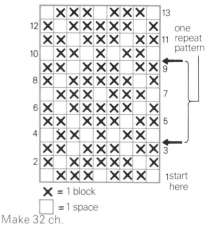

✕ = 1 block
☐ = 1 space

Make 32 ch.

1st row (RS) 1dc into 8th ch from hook, 1dc into each of next 9ch, 2ch, skip 2ch, 1dc into each of next 10dc, 2ch, skip 2ch, 1 dc into last ch. Turn.
Beg with the 2nd row cont to work from chart with pat as set. Even (WS) rows are worked from left to right; uneven (RS) rows from right to left.

Tablecloth and napkins

Serve some instant sunshine for breakfast or any other meal —
with a sunny yellow tablecloth and matching dotted napkins,
all trimmed with delicate filet crochet.

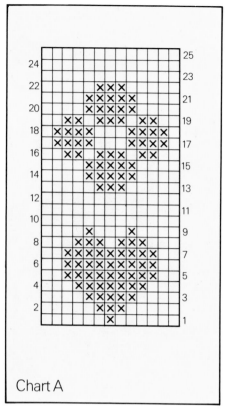

Chart A

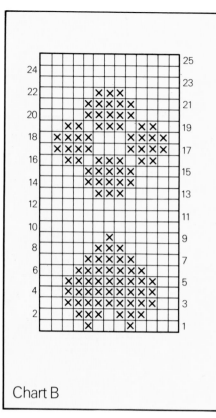

Chart B

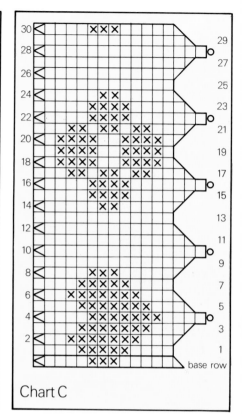

Chart C

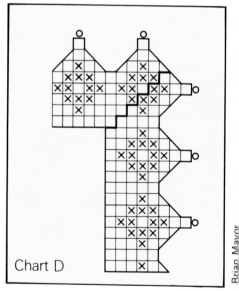

Chart D

Sizes
Tablecloth 56in (142cm) diameter.
Napkins 12in (30cm) square.

Materials
Tablecloth *10oz (250g) of a lightweight mercerized crochet cotton*
Size B (2.50mm) crochet hook
2¾yd (2.5m) of 36in (90cm)-wide cotton fabric
Matching thread
Napkins *(makes 4 edgings)*
3oz(75g) of a lightweight mercerized crochet cotton
Size B (2.50mm) crochet hook
10in (25cm) of 36in (90cm)-wide cotton print fabric
Matching thread

Tablecloth

Insertion
Using size B (2.50mm) hook make 30ch.
Base row 1dc into 6th ch from hook, *1ch, skip next ch, 1dc into next ch, rep from * to end. Turn.
Next row 4th to count as 1dc and 1ch, skip first dc, 1dc into next dc, *1ch, 1dc into next dc, rep from * to end, finishing skip next ch, 1 dc into next ch. Turn.
Following the key, beg with row 1 of chart A, work the 25 rows of heart and flower motifs 4 times. The last flower will be at center of insertion. Beg with row 1 of chart B, work the 25 rows of heart and flower motifs 3 times, then work rows 1 to 11 again. Fasten off. Rejoin yarn to first of center 13 sps on one side and work

4ch, 1 dc into next vertical st, (1ch, 1dc into vertical st) 12 times, turn.
Next row 4ch to count as 1dc and 1ch, skip first dc, 1dc into next dc, *1ch, 1dc into next dc, rep from * to end, finishing skip next ch, 1 dc into next ch. Turn.
Beg with row 1 of chart B, work the 25 rows of heart and flower motifs 3 times, then work rows 1 to 11 again. Fasten off. Rejoin yarn to first of center 13 sps on other side and work as given for first side.

Edging
Using size B (2.50mm) hook make 31 ch.
Base row 1dc into 5th ch from hook, (first dec), (1ch, skip next ch, 1 dc into next ch) 5 times, 1dc into each of next 6ch, (1ch, skip next ch, 1dc into next ch) 4 times, 1ch, skip next ch, 1 sc into last ch. Turn.
Following the key, beg with row 1 of chart C, work the 30 rows of heart and flower motifs 20 times, omitting last row on last repeat. Fasten off.

To finish
Cut 2 semi-circles of fabric 48in (122cm) in diameter, by measuring and marking a point 24in (61cm) down one selvage on wrong side of fabric. Tie one end of string to a thumbtack. Attach a pencil to thread so it is 24in (61cm) from pin. Stick thumbtack into selvage at marked point and draw semi-circle. Cut each semi-circle in half, then, taking ⅝in (1.5cm) hem allowance, hem around outer edge of each quarter. Sew quarters to insertion, then sew edging around hemmed edge.

KEY
☒ = 1 block (3dc plus 1 extra for each additional block)
☐ = 1 space (1dc, 1ch, 1dc)
◺ = work 1sc at end of row instead of 1dc — to curve the work slightly
◿ = inc at end of row by working 1ch, 1dc into same dc as last dc worked; or inc at beg of row by working 4ch, 1dc into inc at beg of row by working 4ch, 1dc into base of 4ch
◻ = dec at end of row by omitting 1ch of next sp, then work 1dc into next dc; or dec at beg of row by working 2ch, then 1 dc into next dc
☐∘ = picot, 4ch, sl st into 3rd ch from hook, 2ch, 1dc into base of 4ch

Brian Mayor

Napkins (makes 4)

Cut four 8¾in (22cm) squares of fabric. Turn up ⅝in (1.5cm) along the edges and hem.

Edging

Using size B (2.50mm) hook make 15ch.
Base row 1dc into 5th ch from hook (first dec), 1ch, skip next ch, 1dc into each of next 3 ch, (1ch, skip next ch, 1 dc into next ch) 3 times. Turn.
Following the key, beg with row 1 of chart D, rep patt until edging fits along one edge of fabric to corner. Now work the mitered corner, working from chart within bold line (so working one space or one block less per row at inside edge) and and at the same time keeping the patt correct at outer edge.
When one half of the corner has been worked turn the chart and work the second half of the corner within the bold line.
When the corner has been completed work from chart until edging fits along second side of fabric, work another corner, then work remaining two sides in the same way.
Sew edging to fabric.

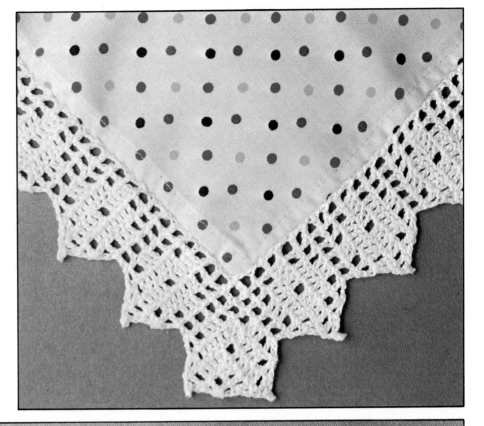

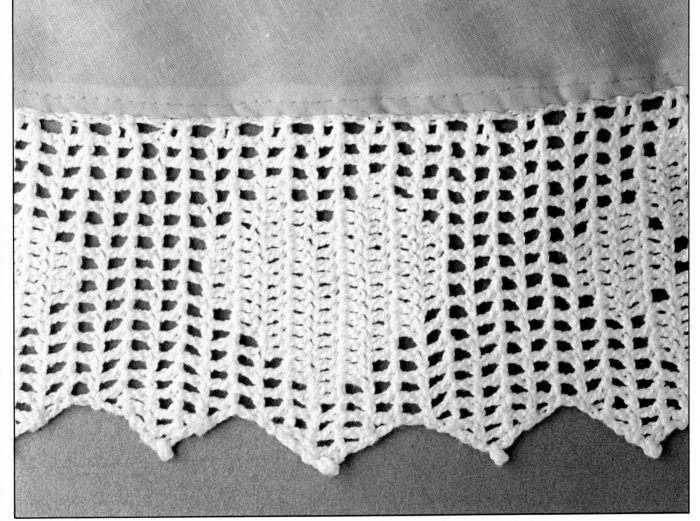

Shoestring

Kitchen cover-ups

Protect your kitchen appliances from dust and grease with these trim slip-on covers.

Finished size

Mixer cover is about 16 × 12½in (40 × 32cm).
Toaster cover is about 12 × 8in (30 × 20cm).
A seam allowance of ¼in (5mm) has been included throughout.

Mixer cover
Materials
- 1¼yd (1.1m) of 36in (90cm)-wide fabric
- 1⅛yd (1m) of 36in (90cm)-wide heavy-weight iron-on interfacing
- 2¼yd (2m) of 1in (2.5cm)-wide bias binding
- 1⅜yd (1.2m) of 2in (5cm)-wide bias binding
- 2¼yd (2m) of narrow filler cord
- Matching thread

1 Cut two pieces of fabric, each 16½ × 13in 42 × 8½in (117 × 21cm) for gusset.
2 From interfacing cut two sides and one gusset the same size as the fabric pieces.
3 Place each interfacing piece shiny side down on wrong side of matching fabric pieces. Iron interfacing in place.

4 Unfold narrow bias binding. Place cord in the center of the binding. Fold binding in half evenly around the cord, wrong side inside and edges matching. Pin and baste along length, close to cord.
5 Place cording on one long edge of gusset with the cord lying inward and the basting ¼in (5mm) in from fabric edge. Pin and baste firmly in place.
6 Repeat step 5 to baste cording to other long edge of gusset.
7 Pin both side pieces together with right sides facing and edges matching. Curve two top corners as follows: at one side mark a point 2in (5cm) in from corner on top edge and another point 2in (5cm) down side edge. Draw a gentle curve from point to point around the corner. Cut along curved line. Separate the sides; re-fold each in half widthwise and trace curve on opposite corner. Cut along curve, and unpin side pieces.
8 Place one piped edge of gusset along side and top edges of one side piece with right sides together and raw edges matching. Pin, baste and stitch in place.
9 Repeat step 8 to join other long edge of gusset to other side piece.

10 Clip into seam allowance around curves on gusset seams. Finish seams. Turn cover right side out.
11 Fold wide bias binding in half evenly over right lower edge of cover, with right side out. Begin binding in center of one side of gusset and pin all around. Turn under the free end and fold it over raw edge at beginning of binding to finish. Baste and topstitch binding in place.

Toaster cover
Materials
- ¾yd (.7m) of 36in (90cm)-wide fabric
- ⅞yd (.8m) of 36in (90cm)-wide heavy-weight iron-on interfacing
- 1¾yd (1.6m) of 1in (2.5cm)-wide bias binding
- 1⅛yd (1m) of 2in (5cm)-wide bias binding; matching thread
- 1¾yd (1.6m) of narrow filler cord

1 Cut two pieces of fabric each 11½ × 7½in (31 × 21cm) for sides. Cut one piece 26 × 7½in (66 × 19cm) for gusset.
2 Make toaster cover as for mixer cover, steps 2 to 11.

Introduction to Tunisian crochet

Tunisian or Afghan crochet, like knitting, probably originated in Arabia. It combines the techniques of knitting and crochet and may well point to an historical link between the two crafts. In fact, the first knitting needles had a hook on one end. As in knitting, loops are made on a long needle, but as in crochet the needle used has a hook on the end and the stitches are worked onto a foundation of chains. The loops are alternately cast on and bound off the needle without turning the work.

Tunisian crochet hooks, like ordinary crochet hooks, come in a range of sizes from sizes B to Q (2.50mm to 10mm), available in 12in (30cm) or 14in (35cm) lengths. The hook is longer than an ordinary crochet hook, since it must accommodate the entire width of the piece being worked.

A variety of strong and elastic fabrics can be produced with Tunisian crochet. This course shows how to work plain Tunisian stitch and later issues will illustrate a number of other stitches, including openwork and color patterns.

Working plain Tunisian stitch

Plain Tunisian stitch, also known as simple, knit and tricot stitch, is the simplest stitch in Tunisian crochet. Once you have mastered it, you should have little difficulty in following other Tunisian crochet stitch patterns. It is best to make your first sample with a hook not smaller than size F (4.00mm) and a sport yarn. This will enable you to see the loops clearly. The yarn and hook are held in the same way as for ordinary crochet.

1 Begin by making a length of chain. Then insert the hook into the top loop only of the second chain from the hook and wind the yarn over the hook as for ordinary crochet.

2 Draw a loop through the chain. There are now 2 loops on the hook.

Frederick Mancini

continued

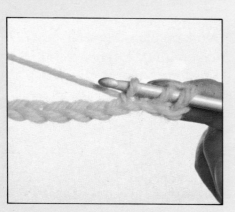

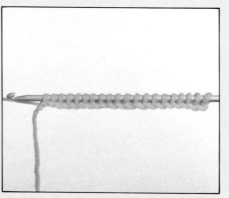

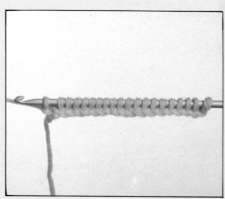

3 Insert the hook into the next chain. Wind the yarn over the hook and draw a loop through. There are now 3 loops on the hook.

4 Continue working from right to left, making loops into each chain and keeping the new loops on the hook to the end of the chain. This completes the first loop row. Do not turn the work.

5 Wind the yarn over the hook and draw it through the first loop on the hook.

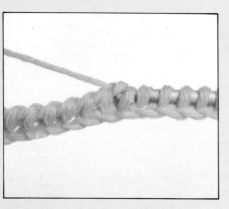

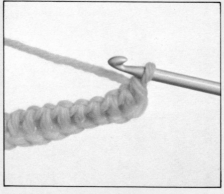

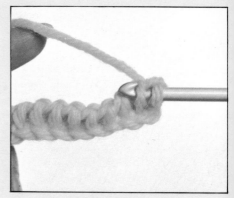

6 Wind the yarn over the hook and draw it through the next two loops on the hook. Continue from left to right, winding the yarn over the hook and drawing it through two loops each time, maintaining an even tension.

7 When there is one loop left on the hook, the return row, which consists of vertical loops connected at the top edge with horizontal chains, has been completed. Do not turn the work.

8 In the next row loops are again picked up across the work from right to left. Keeping the hook at the front of the work, insert the hook from right to left through the *second* vertical loop in the row below, so that it passes behind the strand at the front of the work as shown here.

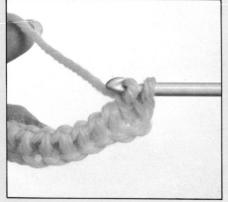

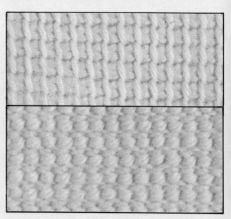

9 Wind the yarn over the hook and draw a loop through. There are now 2 loops on the hook.

10 Working from right to left, make new loops into each of the vertical loops in the row below, inserting the hook from right to left as before behind the last vertical strand at the edge of the work for the last loop.

11 Do not turn; work another return row in the same way from left to right as in steps 5-7. The fabric is made by repeating the loop and return rows. The front has a smooth surface as shown above. The back, shown below, is similar in appearance to reverse stockinette stitch.

Keeping the edges straight

One error you may make with Tunisian crochet is picking up either too few or too many stitches on the loop row. This occurs when you either skip the left side edge stitch or pick up the right-hand edge stitch. Here are some hints that should help the beginner and eliminate the need continually to count the loops on the hook to make sure you have the correct number.

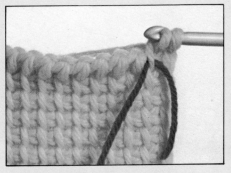

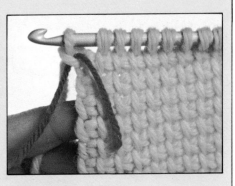

1 The right-hand edge stitch (the first loop of the loop row) is formed by the last loop drawn through on the previous return row. When beginning a loop row insert the hook through the *second* vertical loop below, indicated here with the colored yarn, and never through the first vertical loop.

2 The left-hand edge stitch is formed when the first loop is drawn through on the return row as shown on page 22. It is often pulled up too tightly when the second-to-last stitch in the loop row is worked, making it hard to find. By marking this stitch with a colored thread in the previous row as shown in the picture above, you will become familiar with its position.

Finishing the top of Tunisian crochet

After working a piece of Tunisian crochet to its required length, you should finish the top edge with a row of single crochet before fastening off. This neatens and strengthens the edge and covers the holes which would otherwise be left at the top of the work.

1 Finish the plain Tunisian stitch with a return row so that there is one loop left on the hook. Do not turn the work.

2 Wind the yarn over the hook and draw it through the loop on the hook. This acts as the turning chain.

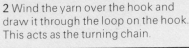

3 Keeping the hook at the front of the work, insert the hook in the usual way from right to left through the second vertical loop in the row below. Wind the yarn over the hook and draw a loop through.

4 Wind the yarn over the hook and draw it through both loops on the hook. This completes the first single crochet.

5 Work single crochet into each vertical strand in the same way to the end of the row. Then cut off yarn and draw it through the last loop. The single crochet pushes the last return row of chains down between the vertical strands, thus filling the space left between the last two rows.

Frederick Mancini

Afghan

A charming introduction to Tunisian crochet—an afghan to keep your knees warm and enliven any room.

Size
55in x 45in (139 x 113cm).

Materials
16oz (440g) of a sport yarn in each of 2 contrasting colors (A and B)
5oz (120g) in contrasting color (C) for joining
Size H (5.00mm) Tunisian crochet hook
Size E (3.50mm) crochet hook

Gauge
19 sts and 38 rows (19 vertical loop rows) to 4in (10cm) worked on size H (5.00mm) Tunisian hook.

To make
Using size H (5.00mm) Tunisian hook and A, make 32ch and work in plain Tunisian stitch (see page 21) working 52 rows (i.e. 26 rows of vertical loops) A, 52 rows B until the 4th stripe in B has been completed. Fasten off.
Make 3 more strips in same way. Now make 4 strips beg with B and working until 4th stripe in A has been completed.

To join strips
Alternating colors, with RS tog, using size E (3.50mm) hook and C, join yarn to first row end of first strip with a sl st, now sl st into first row end of second strip, 1ch, skip next row end on first strip, sl st into next row end, 1ch, skip next row end on second strip, sl st into next row end, cont in this way, working into every alternate row end to end of strips. Fasten off.
Join all strips in this way, alternating the colors.
Now work across stripes thus: With RS facing, using size E (3.50mm) hook and C, join yarn to first vertical loop of 2nd row of second stripe, 1ch, sl st into first vertical loop of 2nd row of first stripe, 1ch, skip next vertical loop on 2nd row of second stripe, sl st into next vertical loop, 1ch, skip next vertical loop of 2nd row of first stripe, sl st into next vertical loop, 1ch, cont in this way, working into every alternate vertical loop to end of strips. Fasten off. Work across all strips in same way.

Edging
With RS facing, using size E (3.50mm) hook, join C to one corner and work 1sc into each row end to corner, 3sc into corner, then work *1sc into each of next 4 sps, (insert hook into next sp, yo and draw a loop through) twice, yo and draw a loop through) twice, yo and draw through 2 loops on hook—1sc decreased —*, rep from * to * to corner, 3sc into corner, 1sc into each row end to corner, 3sc into corner, now work from * to * to corner, 3sc into corner, sl st into first sc.
Next 2 rounds Work 1sc into each sc and 2sc into 2 corner sts all around, sl st into first sc. Fasten off.

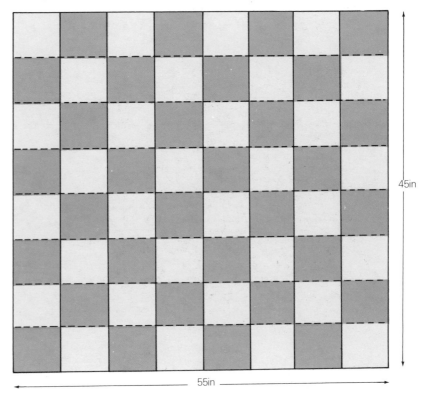

55in

45in

Crochet / COURSE 65

Yarns and textures in Tunisian crochet

Tunisian crochet is often falsely thought to produce only a coarse, bulky and rather unattractive fabric. This mis-apprehension was reinforced in the 19th century, when people used the technique mainly for bulky mufflers, shawls and counterpanes. Plain Tunisian stitch does produce a fabric which can be much thicker than ordinary knitted stockinette stitch or single crochet, making it very suitable for warm garments. But this should not give you the idea that it must always be tightly worked in thick yarns. The versatility of the fabric made by even simple Tunisian crochet stitches can be seen plainly in the samples shown here.

They are worked loosely and tightly in thin and thick yarns to produce both delicate and bulky textures. The following step-by-step instructions illustrate the versatility of this kind of crochet and show you how to work two simple Tunisian crochet stitches and how to introduce new yarn into the fabric.

Tunisian purl stitch

There are two ways of producing the Tunisian purl stitch. In one method the hook is inserted through the vertical loops from left to right downward. The resulting vertical strands slant to the left. In the simpler method given here, however, the hook is inserted from the right. This twists the loops and slants them to the right. As in most Tunisian crochet stitches, the return row for purl stitch is the same as that for plain stitch.

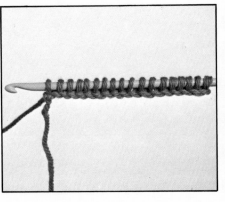

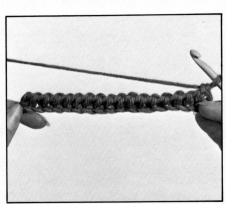

1 Make a length of chain. Insert the hook into the 2nd chain from the hook. Wind the yarn over the hook and draw a loop through. Make loops in this way into each chain to the end. Do not turn the work.

2 Wind the yarn over the hook and draw it through one loop on the hook. Wind the yarn over the hook and draw it through 2 loops on the hook. Then draw through 2 loops at a time to the end of the row. Do not turn the work.

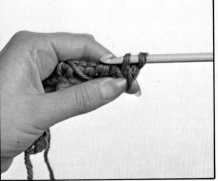

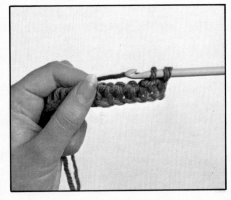

3 On the next row hold the yarn forward to the front of the work. You may find it easier when making the purl loops to hold the yarn in place with the left thumb until the loop is drawn through.

4 Insert the hook from right to left through the second vertical loop in the row below.

5 Wind the yarn over the hook and draw a loop through. Do not pull the yarn through too tightly, as this has the effect of tightening the next vertical loop.

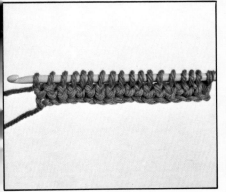

6 Continue working to the end of the row, keeping the yarn at the front of the work and making loops into each vertical strand in the row below. Draw the last loop through the vertical loop at the edge of the work in the same way as when working plain Tunisian stitch (see page 22).

7 Do not turn, but work another return row from left to right as in step 2. To form a Tunisian purl stitch fabric, continue making loop and return rows following steps 2-7.

8 To finish the top edge make one turning chain at the beginning of a loop row. Then with the yarn to the front, insert the hook into the 2nd vertical loop below. Wind the yarn over the hook.

Frederick Mancini

continued

9 Draw a loop through. Wind the yarn over the hook and draw through both loops on the hook, so working one single crochet. Continue working a single crochet into each loop in this way to the end of the row, working the last single crochet through the vertical loop at the edge of the work as when working a loop row, as shown in step 6.

10 Here we show the front of the purl stitch fabric, which has a more textured surface than that of plain stitch.

11 The back of the fabric (shown here) is similar in appearance to knitted garter stitch and could easily be used as the right side of the fabric.

Tunisian stockinette stitch

As its name implies this stitch is very similar in appearance to knitted stockinette stitch. Because of the way the yarn is drawn through the loops, the fabric is drawn up much tighter than that of plain stitch. So you will probably find that you will need to use a larger hook for this stitch. Begin by working a foundation chain, then following steps 1 and 2 of purl stitch (page 27) work 2 rows.

1 At the beginning of the third row insert the hook from front to back through the second vertical loop in the row below. Be sure that the hook is inserted under the chain which lies vertically across the top of the previous return row as it passes through the vertical loop.

2 Wind the yarn over the hook and draw a loop through.

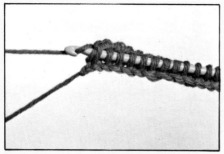

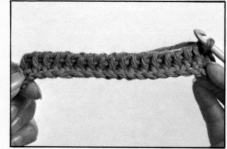

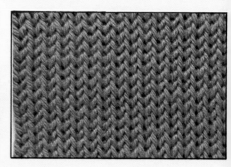

3 Continue making loops in this way, inserting the hook from front to back through each vertical loop to the end of the row, inserting the hook through the center of the last loop at the edge of the work, making sure that there are *two* vertical strands of yarn on the hook at the extreme left-hand edge, to form a firm edge.

4 Do not turn the work. Make a return row from left to right as in step 2 for purl stitch (see page 27).

5 Continue making loop and return rows in this way to form the fabric until it is the required length. Then work single crochet across the top, inserting the hook from front to back through the vertical loop below for each stitch. The fabric is even thicker than plain or purl stitch. If it tends to curl, press gently with a warm iron and a damp cloth.

Introducing new yarn

In Tunisian crochet new yarn should be added at the beginning of a row. The method shown here can be used either for starting a new ball of yarn when one ball has run out or for joining in a new color for stripes. It works equally well for most Tunisian crochet stitches but is shown here with plain stitch.

1 At the end of a return row work all the loops off the hook except the last two. This last chain makes the right-hand edge stitch for the next row so the new yarn should be started here.

2 Drop the old yarn. Wind the new yarn over the hook leaving a long loose end and draw it through the two loops on the hook. Hold the loose end of new yarn along the top of the row below.

3 Insert the hook from right to left through the second vertical loop in the row below. Pass it up *under* the loose end and then wind the working end of the yarn over the hook.

4 Draw the loop through. Insert the hook into the next vertical loop then pass it up *over* the loose end to hold the yarn in place.

5 Continue in this way, passing the hook alternately under and over the loose end with each stitch. Cut the yarn as close to the fabric as possible once it has been woven firmly into the wrong side as shown here.

6 When using the yarn at a later stage in the pattern you can carry it up the side of the work. Change the yarn by drawing the new yarn through the last two loops of the return row as before.

7 Now take the old yarn over the top of the new yarn, bringing the new yarn up to the working position so that the old yarn is looped over the new. It will be held in place once the next stitch has been worked.

8 Continue to loop the old yarn over the new at the beginning of each loop row until it is needed again, drawing it through the last 2 loops of a return row to introduce it once more into the fabric. Here we show you the wrong side of the work with the spare yarn carried neatly up the side and introduced once more into the fabric.

Two teenagers' jackets

Once you have mastered Tunisian purl stitch, these jackets will be easy to make, and the clever use of color makes them a bit special.

Two-color jacket

Sizes
To suit 30[32:34]in (76[83:87]cm) bust.
Length, 24in (60cm).
Sleeve seam, 24in (60cm) with cuff.

Note: Directions for larger sizes are in brackets [ ]; if there is only one set of figures it applies to all sizes.

Materials
25[27:27]oz (700[750:750]g) of a bulky-weight yarn in main color (A)
22[22:24]oz (600[600:650]g) in contrasting color (B)
Size I (6.00mm) Tunisian crochet hook
Size H (5.50mm) crochet hook
6 toggles

Gauge
13 sts and 20 rows to 4in (10cm) worked on size I (6.00mm) hook.

Back
Using size I (6.00mm) Tunisian hook and B, make 56[60:64]ch.
Cont in Tunisian purl st (see page 27) for 8in (20cm). Cut off B. Join on A and work 8in (20cm). Cut off A. Join on B and work 8in (20cm). Fasten off.

Fronts (both alike)
Using size I (6.00mm) hook and B, make 27[29:31]ch and work as for back.

Sleeves
Using size I (6.00mm) hook and A, make 52ch. Work in Tunisian purl for 8in (20cm). Fasten off and turn work to reverse for turn-back cuff. Join on B and work 8in (20cm). Cut off B. Join on A and work a further 8in (20cm). Fasten off.

Hood
Using size I (6.00mm) hook and A, make 67ch. Cont in Tunisian purl st for 13¾in (35cm). Fasten off. Fold in half and join seam.

Front borders (alike)
Using size H (5.50mm) hook, A and with RS facing, work in sc up front edge, working 1sc into each pair of rows, turn and cont in sc for 1¾in (4cm). Fasten off.

To finish
Do not press. Join shoulder seams, leaving approx 8in (20cm) open at center for neck. Placing center of sleeves to shoulder seams, set in sleeves, then join side and sleeve seams, reversing seam on cuff. Sew hood to neck edge. Sew 3 pairs of toggles to front edges and make loops to fasten.

Multi-colored jacket

Sizes
To suit 30[32:34]in (76[83:87]cm) bust.
Length, 24in (60cm).
Sleeve seam, 24in (60cm) with cuff.

Note: Directions for larger sizes are in brackets [ ]; if there is only one set of figures it applies to all sizes.

Materials
16[18:20]oz (450[500:550]g) of a bulky-weight yarn in main color (A)
8[8:10]oz (200[200:250]g) in each of 2 contrasting colors (B and C)
6[6:8]oz (150[150:200]g) in each of 2 contrasting colors (D and E)
Size I (6.00mm) Tunisian crochet hook
Size H (5.50mm) crochet hook
6 toggles

Gauge
13 sts and 20 rows to 4in (10cm) worked on size I (6.00mm) hook.

Back
Using size I (6.00mm) hook and C, make 56[60:64]ch. Cont in Tunisian purl st (see page 27) working 6in (15cm) each in C, B, E and D. Fasten off.

Left front
Using size I (6.00mm) hook and E, make 27[29:31]ch. In Tunisian purl st work 6in (15cm) each in E, A, B and C. Fasten off.

Right front
Using size I (6.00mm) crochet hook and C, make 27[29:31]ch. Cont in Tunisian purl st working 6in (15cm) each in C, D, A and E. Fasten off.

Right sleeve
Using size I (6.00mm) hook and A, make 52ch and work in Tunisian purl st for 8in (20cm). Fasten off and turn work to reverse for turn-back cuff. Rejoin A and work 4in (10cm), then work 6in (15cm) each in C and B. Fasten off.

Left sleeve
Using size I (6.00mm) hook and A, make 52ch and work in Tunisian purl st for 8in (20cm). Fasten off and turn work to reverse for turn-back cuff. Join on B and work 4in (10cm), then work 6in (15cm) each in D and A. Fasten off.

Hood
As two-color jacket.

Front borders
As two-color jacket.

To finish
As two-color jacket.

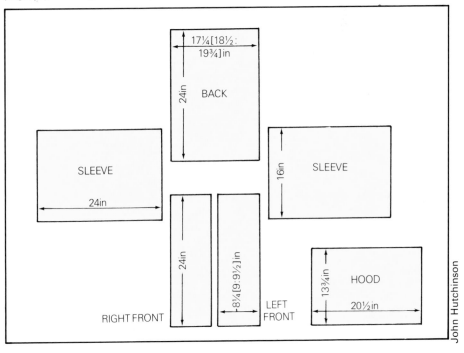

John Hutchinson

*Knitting in rounds to make a flat circle
*Knitting in rounds to make a multi-sided shape
*Patterns for pillow covers

Knitting in rounds to make a flat circle

The shapes produced by flat circular knitting are also known as medallions. To make a medallion, begin knitting at the center of the shape, using a set of 4 needles, since there are so few stitches, and increase outward toward the circumference. Increasing is important in building up a medallion: a number of the methods have been discussed in previous issues. All circles must have at least eight increase points at regular intervals in each increase round.

Keep the circular fabric flat. Experiment to find the number of plain rounds needed between increase rounds. If the medallion becomes ruffly, you are increasing too quickly and need extra plain rounds; subtract plain rounds if the work is tight and conical.

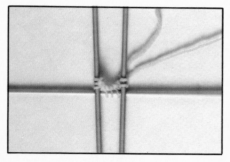

1 Using the two-needle method, cast 8 stitches onto one of the four needles. Knit all the stitches through the back of the loop: this keeps the center flat. Divide the stitches onto 3 needles with 3 stitches on each of 2 needles and 2 stitches on the 3rd.

2 Arrange the needles into a triangular shape, making sure that the stitches do not twist. This is a difficult process as there are so few stitches on the needles. Tie a marker loop of contrasting-colored yarn to left-hand end of stitches to denote beginning of new rounds.

3 Always slipping the marker loop onto the 4th (or spare) needle at the beginning of a round, work first round: K into front and back of each st—called inc 1—to double number of stitches to 16.

4 Work 2 plain rounds in stockinette stitch between each increase round. You may need more or fewer plain rounds according to the thickness of the yarn and the needles being used. Repeat the same number of plain rounds throughout.

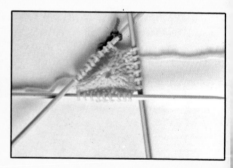

5 Continue with the 4th round: (Inc 1, K1) to end. 24 sts. Note that 8 stitches are increased each time. Work 2 plain rounds.

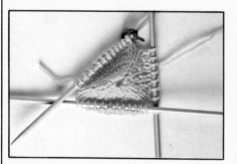

6 Work the 7th round: K1, (inc 1, K2) to last 2 sts, inc 1, K1. 32 sts. Always increase into alternate stitches of pairs of increases in previous increase round.

7 Work the 10th round: K1, (inc 1, K3) to last 3 sts, inc 1, K2. 40 sts. Work 2 plain rounds.

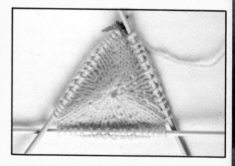

8 Work the 13th round: K2, (inc 1, K4) to last 3 sts, inc 1, K2. 48 sts. Work 2 plain rounds.

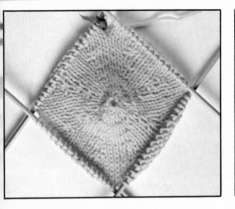

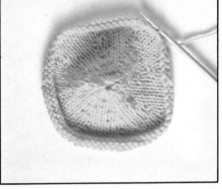

9 Continue increasing in this way, knitting 2, then 3 stitches twice, 4 stitches twice and so on at the start of an increase round, until the circle is the required size. As the stitches become crowded on the original needles, you can introduce more needles from another set or transfer all the stitches to a circular needle if you are making a large circle and have enough stitches to fill a circular needle.

10 Bind off in the usual way after 2 plain rounds have been completed. To make a neat finish at the joining of the rounds, leave the last loop on the needle. Use the needle to pick up a loop from the first bound-off stitch; slip the first loop over the second and draw the cut end of yarn through in the usual way.

11 The finished circle is a flat disk of solid knitting with the increases distributed so that they are unobtrusive. Any small hole in the center of the circle can be pulled together with embroidery stitches using the long end of yarn from casting on.

Knitting in rounds to make a multi-sided shape

In a similar way to making flat circles, you can knit in rounds to produce various geometric shapes (or medallions) including triangles, squares, pentagons, hexagons and octagons. You can make a number of small medallions and join them together in a patchwork fashion to make a larger fabric; or use an extra-large medallion shape as a shawl or tablecloth.

Again, increasing is vital in building up a shape. There are two main methods of increasing to produce similarly-shaped, but different-looking medallions: geometric increasing and bias increasing.

Geometric increasing must be worked at each side of "ribs" radiating from the center of the shape outward. For example, a square has four sides with four radial "ribs": there must be eight increase points on this figure—one on each side of each rib.

Bias increasing has only one increase at each radial point. Instead of lying in a straight line the ribs are turned by the increases to form a clockwise or counter-clockwise spiral pattern.

Geometric increasing

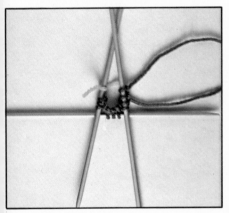

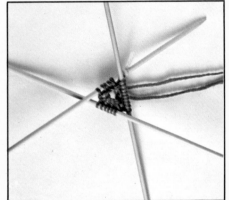

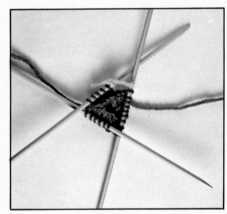

1 Cast onto one of a set of four needles 2 stitches for each side of the shape you are making (i.e. 10 stitches for each of the five sides of the pentagon shown on page 34).
Work first 2 steps as given for making a flat circle, dividing the cast-on stitches so that there are 3 stitches on each of 2 needles and 4 on the third.

2 Always slipping the marker loop onto the 4th (or spare) needle at the beginning of a round, work first round: (K1, pick up loop lying between needles and K tbl— called M1) to end. 10 stitches have been increased making 20 in all.

3 Work the required number of plain rounds between increase ones; see step 4 of making a flat circle.

continued

Fred Mancini

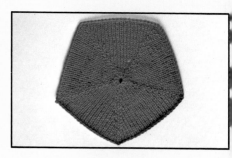

4 Continue with the 4th round: (K1, M1, K3, M1) to end. 30 sts. 10 stitches must always be increased. Later on, as the number of stitches grows, you can introduce extra needles from another set, or transfer all the stitches to a circular needle if there are enough.

5 Work the 7th round: (K1, M1, K5, M1) to end. 40 sts. Work 2 plain rounds. As the medallion grows you can see that the single knit stitches separating increase points form the radial ribs of the shape.

6 Continue in this way, working 2 more stitches in each section between increases on every increase round, until the shape is the required size. Bind off as instructed in step 10 of making a flat circle.

Bias increasing

1 Cast on 10 stitches for a pentagon, then work as given for step 1 of geometric increasing. Work first inc round: (K1, yo, K1) to end. 15 sts. The "yo" makes a small, lacy hole in the fabric and gives the finished shape a decorative appearance.

2 You need few plain rounds with this method as you are increasing slowly: with thicker yarns you may even need to increase on every round. Work 2nd inc round: (K2, yo, K1) to end. 20 sts. 3rd inc round: (K3, yo, K1) to end. 25 sts.

3 Continue to increase one stitch in each of the 5 sections in this way until the pentagon is the required size. The lines of decorative increase swirl outward from the center although the outline of the finished shape is the same as the pentagon formed by geometric shaping.

Pillow covers

The yarns and stitches used to make these pillow covers give a variety of colors and textures to any setting.

Maroon textured pillow cover

Size
Approximately 15in (40cm) in diameter.

Materials
4oz (100g) of a sport yarn in main color (A)
2oz (50g) in each of 2 contrasting colors (B and C)
One set each of four Nos. 6 and 7 (4½ and 5mm) double-pointed knitting needles
Nos. 6 and 7 (4½ and 5mm) circular knitting needles
Circular pillow form, 16in (40cm) in diameter

Gauge
22 sts and 28 rows to 4in (10cm) in patt on No. 7 (5mm) needles.

Pillow cover
Using two No. 6 (4½mm) needles and C, cast on 6 sts.
1st row P into front and back of each st. 12 sts.
2nd row P.
Arrange these sts on 3 needles and cont in patt using 4th needle to work with.
1st round *P1, pick up loop lying between needles and P tbl—called pup—, P2, rep from * to end. 16 sts.
2nd round *P1, (P1, K1, P1, K1) all into next st, turn and K4, turn and P4, turn and K4, pass 2nd, 3rd and 4th sts over first st—called make bobble or MB—, P2, rep from * to end.
3rd round *P1, pup, P3, rep from * to end.
4th round P.
5th round *P1, pup, P4, rep from * to end.
6th round P. 24 sts.
Change to No. 7 (5mm) needles.
7th round *K2 A, 1 B, rep from * to end.
8th round *K1 A, with A pick up loop

lying between needles and K tbl—called puk—, K1 A, 1 B, rep from * to end.
9th round K1 A, *1 B, 3 A, rep from * to last 3 sts, 1 B, 2 A.
10th round K1 A, with A puk, *K1 B, 3 A, with A puk, rep from * to last 3 sts, 1 B, 2 A. 40 sts.
11th round *K4 A, 1 B, rep from * to end.
12th round *K2 A, with A puk, K2 A, 1 B, rep from * to end. 48 sts.
Change to No. 6 (4½mm) needles and C.
13th round K.
14th round P.
15th round As 1st.
16th round As 2nd.
17th round As 3rd.
18th round As 4th.
19th round As 5th. 96 sts.
Change to No. 7 (5mm) needles.
20th round As 7th.
21st round As 8th.
22nd round As 9th.
23rd round As 10th.
24th round As 11th. 160 sts.
25th round As 11th.
Change to No. 6 (4½mm) needles or No. 6 (4½mm) circular needle and C.

Brian Nash

26th round K.
27th and 28th rounds P.
29th round *P1, MB, P2, rep from * to end.
30th-32nd rounds P.
Change to No. 7 (5mm) needles or No. 7 (5mm) circular needle.
33rd round As 7th round, ending K2 tog. 159 sts.
34th round As 8th.
35th round As 9th.
36th round As 10th.
37th round As 11th.
38th round As 11th. 265 sts.
Change to No. 6 (4½mm) needles or No. 6 (4½mm) circular needle and C.
39th round K2 tog, then K to end. 264 sts.
40th and 41st rounds P.
42nd round As 29th.
43rd-45th rounds P.
Bind off in C. Work second piece in same way.

To finish
Join 2 pieces of cover leaving an opening for pillow form. Insert pillow form, then join the opening.

Hexagonal tweed pillow cover

Size
Approximately 14in (35cm) in diameter.

Materials
6oz (150g) of a flecked knitting worsted
Set of four No. 5 (4mm) double-pointed knitting needles
No. 5 (4mm) circular knitting needle
1yd (.9m) unbleached muslin; stuffing

Gauge
22 sts and 32 rows to 4in (10cm) in patt on No. 5 (4mm) needles.

Pillow cover
Using two No. 5 (4mm) needles, cast on 6 sts.
1st row K to end.
2nd row *K1, pick up loop lying between needles and K tbl—called make 1 or M1—, rep from * to last st, K1, then inc 1 by K into st immediately below last st worked. 12 sts. Arrange these sts on 3 needles and use 4th needle to work with. Cont in patt in rounds.
1st round K to end.
2nd round *K1, M1, K1, rep from * to end. 18 sts.
3rd round K to end.
4th round *K1, M1, K1, M1, K1, rep from * to end. 30 sts.
5th round *K1, P3, K1, rep from * to end. Changing to a circular needle when possible, cont to inc in this way at each side of 6 radial ribs on next and every foll 3rd row 17 times in all (234 sts), at same time work in patt of 6 rounds stockinette st, then 6 rounds reverse stockinette st between 2 rib sts. Cont straight until a band of reverse stockinette st is complete. Bind off. Work a 2nd piece.

To finish
Make pillow form from muslin. Use knitting as pattern; make pillow 1in (2.5cm) larger. Stuff. Join 2 sides of knitting, insert pillow form, join rem 2 sides.

Pentagonal striped pillow cover

Size
Approximately 21in (53cm) in diameter.

Materials
2oz (50g) of a knitting worsted in each of 6 colors
Set of four No. 7 (5mm) double-pointed knitting needles
No. 7 (5mm) circular knitting needle
1¼yd (1.2m) unbleached muslin; stuffing

Gauge
21 sts and 28 rows to 4in (10cm) in stockinette st on No. 7 (5mm) needles.

Pillow cover
Using two No. 7 (5mm) needles and one color, cast on 5 sts. Working in stockinette st and stripe sequence of 6 rounds in each color, cont as foll:
1st row K to end.
2nd row K into front and back of each st. 10 sts.
Arrange these sts on 3 needles and use 4th needle to work with. Cont in rounds.
1st and foll alternate rounds K to end.
2nd round *K1, pick up loop lying between needles and K tbl—called make 1

or M1 –, K1, rep from * to end. 15 sts.
4th round *K1, (M1, K1) twice, rep from * to end. 25 sts.
6th round *K1, M1, K3, M1, K1, rep from * to end. 35 sts.
8th round *K1, M1, K5, M1, K1, rep from * to end. 45 sts.
Cont in this way, inc 10 sts on alternate rounds, for 72 rounds. Bind off.
Work a second piece in the same way.

To finish
Make pillow form as for tweed pillow. Join cover, inserting pillow form.

Pillow cover with bobbles

Size
Approximately 16in (40cm) in diameter.

Materials
*8oz (200g) of a knitting worsted
Set of four No. 6 (4½mm) double-pointed knitting needles
No. 6 (4½mm) circular needle
Circular pillow form, 16in (40cm) in diameter*

Gauge
21 sts and 32 rows to 4in (10cm) in stockinette st on No. 6 (4½mm) needles.

Pillow cover
Using two No. 6 (4½mm) needles cast on 4 sts.
1st row K into front and back of each st. 8 sts.
Arrange these sts on 3 needles and cont in rounds, working with 4th needle.
1st round K into front and back of each st. 16 sts.
2nd round *K2, pick up loop lying between needles and K tbl – called make 1 or M1 –, rep from * to end. 24 sts.
3rd round *K3, P3, rep from * to end.
4th round *K3, M1, P3, M1, rep from * to end. 32 sts.
5th round *K4, P4, rep from * to end.
6th round *K4, M1, P4, M1, rep from * to end. 40 sts.
7th round *K5, P2, (P1, K1, P1, K1) all into next st, turn and K4, turn and P4, turn and K4, pass 2nd, 3rd and 4th sts over first st – called make bobble or MB –, P2, rep from * to end.
8th round *K5, M1, P5, M1, rep from * to end. 48 sts.
9th round *K6, P6, rep from * to end.
10th round *K6, M1, P6, M1, rep from * to end. 56 sts.
11th round *K7, P7, rep from * to end.
12th round *K7, M1, P7, M1, rep from * to end. 64 sts.
13th round *K8, P8, rep from * to end.
14th round *K8, M1, P8, M1, rep from * to end. 72 sts.
15th round *K9, P2, MB, P3, MB, P2, rep from * to end.
Cont in this way, inc as set on alternate rounds and working bobbles in alternating

spaces on reverse stockinette st sections only on every foll 8th row, until cover measures 16in (40cm). Bind off. Work a second piece.

To finish
As maroon pillow cover.

Yellow and pink pillow cover

Size
Approximately 22in (56cm) along lower edge.

Materials
*4oz (100g) of a knitting worsted in each of 2 contrasting colors (A and B)
Set of four No. 7 (5mm) double-pointed knitting needles
No. 7 (5mm) circular knitting needle
1⅜yd (1.3m) unbleached muslin; stuffing*

Gauge
20 sts and 28 rows to 4in (10cm) in stockinette st on No. 7 (5mm) needles.

Pillow cover
Using two No. 7 (5mm) needles and A. cast on 7 sts.
1st row K twice into each st to end. 14 sts.
2nd and 3rd rows K.
4th row *K1, pick up loop lying between needles and work into back of it – called make one or M1 –, rep from * to end. 28 sts.
Arrange these sts on 3 needles and cont in stockinette st working with 4th needle.
1st and 2nd rounds K.
3rd round *K2, M1, rep from * all around. 42 sts.
4th and 5th rounds K.
6th round *K3, M1, rep from * all around 56 sts.
7th and 8th rounds K.
9th round *K4, M1, rep from * all around. 70 sts.
10th and 11th rounds K.
12th round *K5, M1, rep from * all around. 84 sts.
13th and 14th rounds K.
Cont to inc in this way until the radius is 5½in (14cm). Change to B and cont for a further 5½in (14cm) inc as before: diameter of cover is 22in (56cm). Bind off.

To finish
Fold cover in half and join seam, leaving an opening. Use folded cover as pattern for pillow form and make it from muslin and stuffing. Insert pillow form and close opening.

Cream pillow cover

Size
Approximately 22in (55cm) in diameter.

Materials
*11oz (300g) of a knitting worsted
Set of four No. 7 (5mm) double-pointed knitting needles
No. 7 (5mm) circular knitting needle
1⅜yd (1.3m) unbleached muslin; stuffing*

Gauge
20 sts and 28 rows to 4in (10cm) in stockinette st on No. 7 (5mm) needles.

Pillow cover
Using two No. 7 (5mm) needles cast on 6 sts and K 1 row.
Next row K twice into each st to end. 12 sts.
Next row K.
Next row K twice into each st to end. 24 sts.
Arrange these sts on 3 needles and beg flower motif working with 4th needle.
1st round K.
2nd round *P1, yo, (K1, yo) twice, K1, yo, rep from * 5 times more.
3rd round *P2, K2, yo, K1, yo, K2, P1, rep from * 5 times more.
4th round *P1, yo, P1, K3, yo, K1, yo, K3, P1, yo, rep from * 5 times more.
5th round *P3, K4, yo, K1, yo, K4, P2, rep from * 5 times more.
6th round *P1, yo, P2, K5, yo, K1, yo, K5, P2, yo, rep from * 5 times more.
7th round *P3, K6, yo, K1, yo, K6, P2, rep from * 5 times more.
8th round *P1, yo, P3, K7, yo, K1, yo, K7, P3, yo, rep from * 5 times more.
9th round *P5, K2 tog tbl, K13, K2, tog, P4, rep from * 5 times more.
10th round *P1, yo, P4, K15, P4, yo, rep from * 5 times more.
11th round *P6, K2 tog tbl, K11, K2 tog, P5, rep from * 5 times more.
12th round *P1, yo, P5, K13, P5, yo, rep from * 5 times more.
13th round *P7, K2 tog tbl, K9, K2 tog, P6, rep from * 5 times more.
Cont to dec in this way at the end of each petal on every alternate round 4 times more, cont to inc as set on alternate rows until the 22nd round has been completed.
Next round *P12, sl 1, K2 tog, psso, P11, rep from * 5 times more.
Cont to work inc as before on every alternate round and P all sts in between dec on 11th and foll 10th rounds thus:
1st dec round *P1, yo, P15, P3 tog, P15, yo, rep from * all around.
2nd dec round *P1, yo, P19, P3 tog, P19, yo, rep from * all around.
3rd dec around *P1, yo, P23, P2 tog, P23, yo, rep from * all around.
4th dec round *P1, yo, P27, P3 tog, P27, yo, rep from * all around.
P5 more rounds. Bind off.
Work a second piece in the same way.

To finish
Make pillow form as for tweed pillow. Join 2 pieces of cover, inserting pillow.

Trimming pockets with a flap

Pocket flaps can be merely decorative—to give the impression of a mock pocket—or practical covers for openings, especially when fastened down with a button. Both inserted and patch pockets can be trimmed with flaps. With an inserted pocket it is best to sew the flap on after-ward; otherwise you would need to knit it in at the same time as the pocket, which is impractical. However, as a patch pocket is sewn on when the garment is complete, you can knit the flap into the fabric at the required position. Further information about working inserted pockets are in Volume 5, page 42 and patch pockets are discussed in Volume 4, page 33.

The flap is usually made in the same fabric as the waistbands and cuffs; if the garment has stockinette stitch hems, the flap should be in a double fabric to face and finish the raw edges.

Inserted pocket with a separate flap

1 When working an inserted pocket, you first make a separate lining, leaving the stitches on a holder. Work the main fabric to the position of the pocket opening, then bind off the stitches (these must equal the stitches in the lining). Replace the bound-off stitches by knitting in the lining.

2 After completing the main fabric, make the pocket flap as directed in the instructions. This is the flap for the Shetland pattern jacket on page 40: it is triangular with a buttonhole and a few straight rows at the top which has slightly more stitches than the opening. The fabric is double to complement the collar, lower band and cuffs and gives a neat, solid finish to the edges.

3 Complete the triangular flap by placing the right sides of the double fabric together. Sew along 2 shaped sides, leaving the top edges and a few rows at the top of the shape open.

4 Turn the flap right side out: the front of the flap is the first side worked with decrease shaping.

5 Attach the flap to the main fabric. With right sides together, place the top edge of the flap just above the bound-off stitches of the pocket opening. Sew along one thickness of the flap (the top side) using a backstitch seam. Roll under the open edge of the underside of the flap and slip stitch it in position to hide the seam underneath completely.

6 Turn the flap down so that it covers the pocket opening. Finish the double buttonhole with buttonhole stitches worked in matching sewing thread. Sew button onto front of pocket, being careful not to stitch through lining as well.

Patch pocket with knitted-in flap

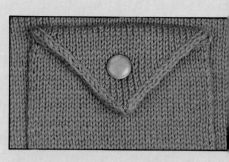

1 Here the pocket is sewn on after the garment is complete, but you can make the flap before beginning the main fabric. The flap in this picture is the same double fabric and triangular shape as that in the Shetland pattern jacket. However, you must cast on with a separate length of yarn (see Volume 8, page 42) and leave the final stitches on the needle, ending with a knit row. Unravel the cast-on edge and pick up the exposed loops with another needle pointing in the same direction as the first.

2 With right sides together, join 2 sides of the flap to within about ⅜in (1cm) of the needles. Turn right side out. Work the main fabric to the position of the top of the pocket, ending with a wrong-side row. Knit the pocket flap into the main fabric on the next row. Hold the needles with the points facing to the right on top of the main fabric on the left-hand needle; knit 3 stitches together across the flap, taking one stitch from each needle.

3 The stitches at the top of the flap are now completely worked into the main fabric, and there is no open edge to finish off, except for the few row ends at the top of the flap, which must be neatly joined. When the fabric is finished, sew on the patch pocket; see knitting course 15, Volume 4, page 33 for further details.

Finishing a gathered edge with a band or cuff

In the same way as adding a cuff when dressmaking, a knitted stockinette stitch band can be used to enclose and finish a gathered edge. The band may be at the lower edge of a blouson-type jacket or may form a cuff at the lower edge of a sleeve.

Normally the band is knitted across a narrow width using a small number of stitches equal to twice the width, so that it can be folded in half to form a double fabric. As the band is knitted widthwise, you can make it the length you wish to fit your measurements: you must remember to leave about 2in (5cm) ease.

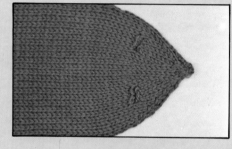

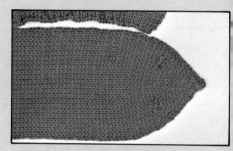

1 Make band to required length. Here is the band for the lower edge of the jacket on page 40. The cast-on stitches form one straight, short end, while the opposite end is pointed to form a neat trimming and has a buttonhole for a fastening.

2 Using sewing thread, work a line of gathering stitches about ⅜in (1cm) up from the lower edge of the jacket or sleeve. Draw up the gathers to fit the band exactly between the short, straight edge and the start of the point shaping.

3 Place right side of band to right side of fabric, matching edges. Even out gathers, then pin and baste in place. Use a backstitch seam, worked about ⅜in (1cm) in from edge, to sew band to fabric. With right sides together, also join short end of band along two sides of pointed end.

4 Turn the point of the band right side out: fold the band in half to the wrong side of the gathered fabric. Using matching yarn—here it is a contrasting color for clarity—slip stitch the band in place exactly on top of the backstitch seam.

5 When the band is completely sewn on, you can finish the buttonhole in the double fabric with buttonhole stitches worked through both thicknesses in matching thread. Sew the button to the center of the straight end of the band as close to the edge as possible.

Shetland patterns

Shetland knitting produces intricately patterned fabrics which are similar to, and often confused with, Fair Isle patterns. Both styles originate in the Shetland Isles, but Shetland designs have a Scandinavian influence from the Norwegians who settled in the islands. Fair Isle patterns often include bands of different designs, whereas a Shetland pattern is an allover pattern: it is characterized by the use of the soft color effects of the natural Shetland yarns—natural, off-white, brown and gray. A bright color is introduced only if it is necessary to highlight part of the pattern.

The techniques involved in a Shetland design are the same as for a Fair Isle one— the entire design is in stockinette stitch, there are only 2 colors in any one row and the color not in use is stranded or woven across the back of the fabric. The designs here are shown in chart form with symbols to denote the colors. For more details of techniques used here see the courses on Fair Isle knitting in Volume 9.

Repeat 12 rows

Repeat 12 sts + 1 extra

Repeat 16 rows

Repeat 16 sts + 1 extra

Repeat 16 rows

Repeats 16sts + 1 extra

Brian Mayor

Mike Berend

rep 6sts

☐ = A
✕ = Medium
○ = Dark
• = Light

24 rows

Woman's Shetland-patterned jacket

A beautiful jacket to knit in soft shades of brown.

Sizes
To fit 32[34:36:38:40]in (83[87:92:97:102]cm) bust.
Length, 25¾[26¼:26½:27:27¼]in (66[67:68:69:70]cm), adjustable.
Sleeve seam, 15¼[15¾:16¼:16½:17]in (39[40:41:42:43]cm).
Note: Directions for larger sizes are in brackets []; if there is only one set of figures it applies to all sizes.

Materials
11[11:13:13:15]oz (300[300:350: 350:400]g) of a sport yarn in main color (A)
4[4:4:6:6]oz (100[100:100:150: 150]g) in each of 3 contrasting colors, (medium, dark and light)
1 pair each Nos. 3 and 6 (3¼ and 4½mm) knitting needles
No. 6 (4½mm) circular knitting needle 22in (56cm) open-ended zipper
5 buttons
Stitch holder

Gauge
22 sts and 30 rows to 4in (10cm) in stockinette st on No. 6 (4½mm) needles (22 sts and approx. 22 rows to 4in [10cm] in patt).

Pocket linings (make 2)
Using No. 6 (4½mm) needles and A, cast on 29 sts. Beg with a K row, work 5in (13cm) stockinette st; end with a P row. Cut off yarn and leave sts on holder.

Back and fronts
Using No. 6 (4½mm) circular needle and A, cast on 205[217:229:241:253] sts. Work in one piece in rows to underarm. Beg with a K row, cont in stockinette st, working in patt from chart, until work measures 6in (15cm); end with a K row.
Place pockets
Next row Patt 12[13:15:16:18] sts, bind off 29, patt to last 41[42:44:45:47] sts, bind off 29, patt to end.
Next row Patt 12[13:15:16:18] sts, K

across sts of one pocket lining from holder, patt to next pocket, K across sts of second pocket lining from holder, patt to end.
Cont in patt until work measures 16in (41cm); end with a P row.
Divide for armholes
Next row Patt 51[54:57:60:63] sts, bind off one st, patt 101[107:113:119:125] sts, bind off one st, patt to end.
Cont on last 51[54:57:60:63] sts for left front until armholes measure 6¼[6¼:6¾:6¾:7]in (16[16:17:17:18]cm); end with a K row.
Shape neck
Bind off 9[9:10:10:10:11] sts at beg of next row, 2[3:3:3:4] sts at beg of foll alternate row and 3 sts at beg of foll 2 alternate rows. Dec one st at end (neck edge) of next and foll 1[1:1:2:1] alternate rows. 32[34:36:38:40] sts. Cont straight until armhole measures 8¼[8¾:9:9½:9¾]in (21[22:23:24:25]cm); end with a P row.
Shape shoulder
Bind off 6[7:7:8:8] sts at beg of next

and foll 3 alternate rows. Work 1 row. Bind off rem 8[6:8:6:8] sts. With WS facing, rejoin yarn to rem 101[107:113: 119:125] sts for back. Cont straight until armholes match front to shoulder; end with a P row.

Shape shoulders
Bind off 6[7:7:8:8] sts at beg of next 8 rows and 8[6:8:6:8] sts at beg of foll 2 rows. Bind off rem 37[39:41:43:45] sts. With WS facing, rejoin yarn to rem 51[54:57:60:63] sts and work to match left front, reversing shaping.

Sleeves
Using No. 6 (4½mm) needles and A, cast on 53[57:59:63:65] sts. Beg with a K row, cont in stockinette st, inc one st at each end of 5th and every foll 7th row until there are 81[85:89:93:97] sts. Cont straight until sleeve measures 15¼[15¾: 16¼:16½:17]in (39[40:41:42:43]cm); end with a P row.

Shape top
Bind off 5 sts at beg of next 12[12:14: 14:16] rows. Bind off rem 21[25:19:23: 17] sts.

Collar
Using No. 3 (3¼mm) needles and A, cast on 37[39:41:45] sts. K 1 row. Cont in stockinette st, cast on 4 sts at beg of next 12 rows. Work 3 rows; end with a P row.
Next row K1, K twice into next st, K to last 3 sts, K twice into next st, K2. Work 3 rows. Rep last 4 rows 6 times more, then work 2 rows.
Next row K1, sl 1, K1, psso, K to last 3 sts, K2 tog, K1.
Work 3 rows. Rep last 4 rows 6 times more, then work 2 rows. Bind off 4 sts at beg of next 12 rows. Bind off rem 37[39:41:45] sts.

Pocket flaps (make 2)
Using No. 3 (3¼mm) needles and A, cast on 33 sts.
1st-4th rows Beg with a K row, work in stockinette st.
5th row K1, sl 1, K1, psso, K to last 3 sts, K2 tog, K1.
6th row P1, P2 tog, P to last 3 sts, P2 tog tbl, P1.
7th row As 5th.
8th row P.
9th-12th rows As 5th-8th. 21 sts.
13th row K1, sl 1, K1, psso, K6, bind off 3 for buttonhole, K to last 3 sts, K2 tog, K1.
14th row As 6th, casting on 3 sts over those bound off on previous row.
Cont to dec as before, at each end of 3 out of every 4 rows, until 3 sts rem; end with a P row.
Next row K twice into each of first 2 sts, K1.
Next row P twice into first st, P to last 2 sts, P twice into next st, P1.
Next row K twice into first st, K to last 2 sts, K twice into next st, K1.

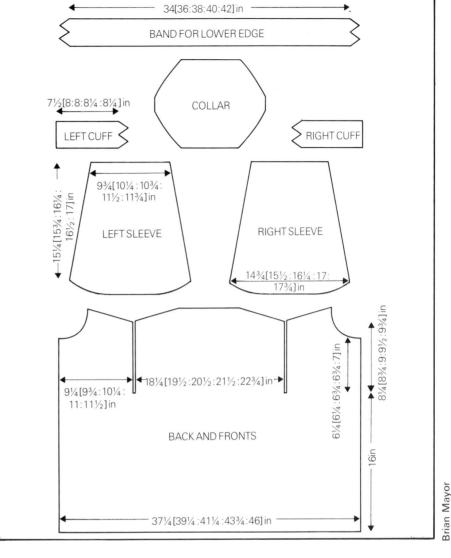

Next row P.
Inc in this way, at each end of 3 out of every 4 rows, until there are 17 sts. Cont to inc, make a buttonhole over center 3 sts of next 2 rows, then cont to inc until there are 33 sts. Work 3 rows. Bind off firmly.

Band for lower edge
Using No. 3 (3¼mm) needles and A, cast on 25 sts. Beg with a K row, work in stockinette st for 34[36:38:40:42]in (86[91:97:102:107]cm); end with a P row.
**Shape point
1st row K5, bind off 3, K to last 8 sts, bind off 3, K to end.
2nd row P to end, casting on 3 sts over those bound off in previous row.
3rd row K1, (sl 1, K1, psso, K7, K2 tog, K1) twice.
4th and every foll alternate row P.
5th row K1, (sl 1, K1, psso, K5, K2 tog, K1) twice.
7th row K1, (sl 1, K1, psso, K3, K2 tog, K1) twice.
9th row K1, (sl 1, K1, psso, K1, K2 tog, K1) twice.

11th row K1, K3 tog, K1, sl 1, K2 tog, psso, K1.
13th row K1, sl 2 knitwise, K1, p2sso, K1. Bind off.
Rejoin yarn to rem 13 sts and work to match first side.

Cuffs (make 2)
Using No. 3 (3¼mm) needles and A, cast on 25 sts. Beg with a K row, work in stockinette st for 7½[8:8:8¼:8¼]in (19[20: 20:21:21]cm); end with a P row. Complete as for lower edge band from ** to end.

To finish
Block. For front edging using No. 3 (3¼mm) needles, A and with RS facing, pick up and K 120 sts along one front edge. Bind off knitwise. Work other edge in same way. Join shoulder and sleeve seams. Set in sleeves. Sew on lower band, fold in half to WS and slip stitch in place. Sew on cuffs. With RS facing, sew bound-off collar edge to neck. Fold to inside, slip stitch in place. Sew down pocket linings, flaps. Attach zipper, buttons.

Shoestring

Homespun lighting

Cover an old lampshade frame with novelty yarn for an unusual and striking effect.

Materials
A Tiffany-style lampshade
13yd (12m) of $\frac{3}{8}$in (1cm)-wide white cotton seam binding
11oz (300g) of a thick, textured yarn
Matching thread
Bodkin

1 Remove old cover from lampshade. Bind each strut of the lampshade frame with seam binding, tucking the ends in at the top and fastening the binding to itself at the bottom.
2 Bind the bottom ring of the lampshade frame with seam binding. At the end, cut the binding, turn under the end and fix it firmly in place by sewing it to the binding on the outside of the ring.
3 Repeat step 2 on the top ring of the lampshade frame.
4 Cut a length of yarn about 6$\frac{1}{2}$yd (6m) long and wind it into a small hank. Beginning at one strut junction, wind the yarn around the bottom ring. Lay the end along the ring and wind the yarn over it to hold it tightly in place. Continue winding the yarn round and round the bottom ring evenly, so that the yarn lies beside itself closely.
5 When you reach the beginning, fasten the end in place on the inside of the frame by sewing the yarn to the yarn on the ring.
6 Repeat steps 4 and 5 to cover the top ring with a length of yarn about 2$\frac{3}{4}$yd (2.5m) long.
7 Cut a length of yarn about 13$\frac{1}{2}$yd (12.5m) long and wind it into a small hank. Wind one end around one strut where it joins the top ring, then take the hank and wind it around the strut next to it. Holding the end in place, wind the yarn round and round these two struts, over the end, keeping the yarn close together and parallel to itself and to the bottom ring.
8 Continue winding until you reach the bottom ring. Sew the end to the last strand of yarn on the inside of the frame and to the yarn on the bottom ring.
9 Repeat steps 7 and 8 on alternate struts around the frame.
10 Repeat steps 7 and 8 on the struts in between the ones already covered. Thread the yarn onto a bodkin to work over these struts so that the yarn can be slotted in between the rows of yarn on each side. Finish off as before.

Malcolm Robertson

*Shaping underarm to start a circular yoke
*Working a circular yoke
*Stitch Wise: Scandinavian patterns
*Patterns for His/Hers Scandinavian ski sweater

Shaping underarm to start a circular yoke

A circular yoke, worked in one piece, is an ideal and easy-fitting top for sportswear; it is also the perfect background for patterns and motifs, since there are no seams that are likely to produce awkward joinings.

Preparation is made for a circular yoke on the separate sections of a garment—back, front and sleeves—before they are joined so that the yoke may be worked.

The back and front of a sweater with a circular yoke are alike. Work in flat knitting as far as the underarm; then work some shaping at the underarm and build up a curved edge across the top of the front or back to prepare it for working around the yoke.

Some top shaping (corresponding to the underarm shaping on the back and front) is worked on the sleeves in the usual way; there is no need to shape a curved edge. The instructions used for the step-by-step photographs here are for the smallest size sweater on page 47.

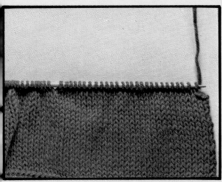

1 Knit the back, or front, to the position of the underarm, ending with a purl row. Over the next few rows, at the same time as decreasing at the armhole edge, you must shape a curved edge from the center outward for the yoke. **1st row** Bind off 2, K until there are 27 sts on right-hand needle, turn. **2nd row** Sl 1, P to end.
Here the first 2 shaping rows are complete.

2 The curved edge is shaped by turning rows, leaving a number of stitches unworked at the inner edge on alternate rows. Here the first 9 shaping rows have been worked (see the pattern for further details).
Complete the first side by working the **10th row** Sl 1, P to end. All the stitches are now on one needle. Cut off the yarn.

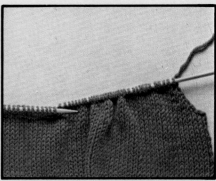

3 With the right side of the work facing and the needle holding the stitches in your left hand, slip the first 34 stitches onto the right-hand needle: this includes all the unworked stitches at the ends of turning rows and 11 stitches in the center unworked from the beginning. Rejoin the yarn to the next stitch and knit to the end of the row.

4 Follow the pattern and shape the other underarm and curved edge to match the first. This is just before the 9th shaping row is worked; all the turning rows at this edge are worked on a purl row.

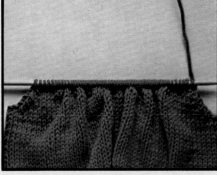

5 Complete the shaped edge by purling across all the stitches: there should be 57 (as some have been decreased at the armhole edges). Cut off the yarn and leave the stitches on a spare needle.

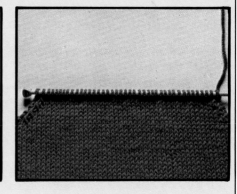

6 Work both the sleeves to same point as the back and front: 10 shaping rows on the sleeve top correspond to the armhole shaping on those sections. Again, cut off the yarn and leave the stitches on a spare needle.

Fred Mancini

Working a circular yoke

A circular knitting needle is a vital piece of equipment for making this type of yoke, because it can carry the large number of stitches in the yoke and allow you to work easily in rounds and follow a pattern at the same time.

The instructions used to demonstrate the basic technique here are again for the smallest size sweater on page 47. Note that the number of rows between each decrease row on the yoke appears to be fairly erratic. However the straight sections between shaping are to accommodate the varying depths of patterned bands in the yoke.

1 Join the separate pieces of knitting on spare needles together on a circular needle. With the right side of each piece facing, start with the back and knit across each piece: work 2 stitches together at each seam. When all 192 stitches are on the circular needle, form it into a circle and knit to the center of the back to start the rounds.

2 Work 10 rounds of stockinette stitch (the garment on page 46 has a zig-zag pattern here). The next round is the first decrease round: you must decrease about an eighth of the total number of stitches evenly around the yoke. Work the **11th round** *K6, K2 tog, rep from * to end. 168 stitches remain.

3 Continue in stockinette stitch for 17 rounds; again this section would probably be patterned on a sweater. The second decrease round is the **29th round** *K5, K2 tog, rep from * to end. 144 stitches remain.

Stitch Wise

Scandinavian patterns

Scandinavian designs come mainly from Norway, Sweden and Denmark. They often feature snowflake motifs, reindeer and folk-lore characters; allover dotted designs make up another popular pattern. The patterns either form an allover fabric or can be worked in bands similar to Fair Isle knitting.

Typical of Norway are border designs in deep colors against a white background with black stripes. Danish borders are usually smaller and in one color against white, while Swedish patterns are often entirely in white on a gray background.

Usually patterned garments are made in thick wool yarn to suit cold climates and the traditional outdoor pastimes of these countries such as skiing and skating. Many designs feature circular yokes (see pages 43-45).

The designs here are shown in chart form with symbols to represent the various colors. Use Fair Isle or jacquard stranding and weaving techniques where appropriate.

Swedish motif

□ = gray
  = white

Norwegian border

□ = white
o = black
x = maroon

4 Continue in stockinette stitch, decreasing on 35th, 46th and 51st rounds by working one less stitch each time between decreases. At the end of the 51st round 72 stitches remain: these stitches are for either a crew neckband or a turtleneck.

5 The remaining stitches are too few to continue in rounds on a circular needle. Change to a set of 4 double-pointed needles; divide the stitches among 3 of the needles and work with the 4th. Work in rounds of K2, P2 ribbing to a depth of $2\frac{1}{4}$in (6cm) for a crew neckband. To avoid making the neck too tight to pull over your head, bind off loosely in ribbing. To ensure an evenly bound-off edge, use a larger needle.

6 The finished yoke is shaped for a comfortable fit and looks most attractive when it is patterned. The only seams you need to join are the few rows of underarm shaping at the base of the yoke. Then join the side and sleeve seams as usual.

Scandinavian reindeer motif

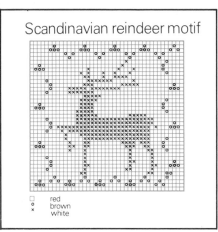

□ red
o brown
× white

Danish borders

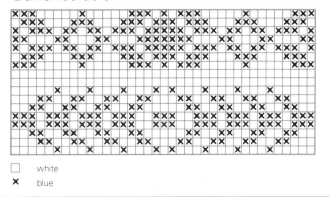

□ white
✗ blue

Nordic style

The perfect sweater for the slopes or après-ski.

Sizes

To fit 32[35:38:41:44]in (81[89:97: 104:112]cm) bust/chest.
Length, 26¼[26¾:27¼:28:29]in (65[67: 69:71:73]cm).
Sleeve seam, 17[17½:17¾:18:18½]in (43[44:45:46:47]cm).
Note Directions for larger sizes are in brackets []; if there is only one set of figures it applies to all sizes.

Materials

24[26:28:30:32]oz (600[650: 700:750:800]g) of a knitting worsted in main color (A)
1[1:2:2:3] balls in contrasting color (B)
1 ball in contrasting color (C)
1 ball in contrasting color (D)
1 pair each Nos. 4 and 6(3¾ and 4½mm) knitting needles
No. 6(4½mm) circular knitting needle
Set of four No. 4(3¾mm) double-pointed needles

Gauge

15 sts and 22 rows to 4in (10cm) in stockinette st on No. 6 (4½mm) needles.

Back

Using No. 4 (3¾mm) needles and A, cast on 70[74:82:86:94] sts.
1st row K2, *P2, K2, rep from * to end.
2nd row P2, *K2, P2, rep from * to end.
Rep these 2 rows for 2½in (6cm); end with 2nd row and dec one st in center of last row. 69[73:81:85:93] sts. Change to No. 6 (4½mm) needles. **Beg with K row, cont in stockinette st. Work 2 rows. Join in B. Work 4 rows patt from chart A. **Cut off B. Cont in stockinette st with A until work measures 15½[15¾:16:16½: 17]in (39[40:41:42:43]cm); end with P row, **at same time** inc one st at each end of first row on 2nd and 4th sizes only, 69[75:81:87:93] sts.
Shape armholes and yoke
1st row Bind off 2, until there are 27[29:31:34:36] sts on right-hand needle, turn.
2nd and foll alternate rows Sl 1, P to end.
3rd row K1, K2 tog, K19[21:23:25:27], turn.
5th row K1, K2 tog, K13[15:17:18:20], turn.
7th row K1, K2 tog, K7[9:11:11:13], turn.
9th row K1, K2 tog, K2[3:4:4:5]. Cut off yarn. Sl 30[33:36:39:42] sts onto right-hand needle, rejoin yarn and K to end. 29[31:33:36:38] sts.
2nd row Cast off 2, P until there are 27[29:31:34:37] sts on right-hand needle, turn.
3rd and foll alternate rows Sl 1, K to last 3 sts, K2 tog tbl, K1.

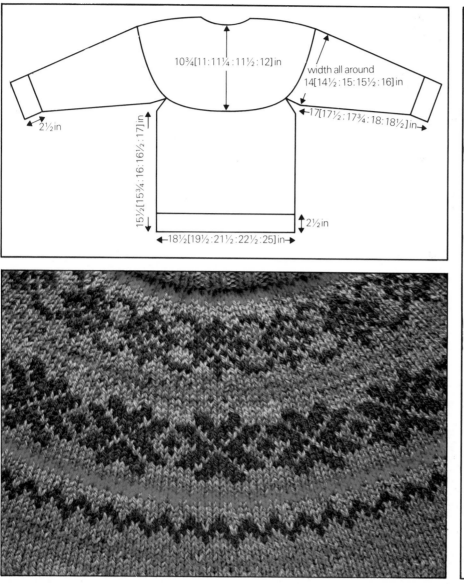

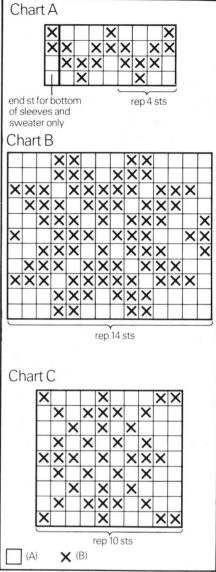

Chart A

end st for bottom
of sleeves and
sweater only

rep 4 sts

Chart B

rep 14 sts

Chart C

rep 10 sts

☐ (A)   ✕ (B)

4th row P21 [23:25:27:29], turn.
6th row P15 [17:19:20:22], turn.
8th row P9 [11:13:13:15], turn.
9th row As 3rd. 57 [63:69:75:81] sts.
10th row P across all sts. Cut off yarn and leave sts for time being.

Front
Work as given for back.

Sleeves
Using No. 4 (3¾mm) needles and A, cast on 34 [34:38:38:42] sts. Rib 2½in (6cm) as for back; end with 2nd row and dec one st in center of last row. 33 [33:37:37:41] sts. Change to No. 6 (4½mm) needles. Work from ** to ** as for back. Cut off B. Cont in stockinette st with A, inc one st at each end of next row on 2nd and 4th sizes only, then at each end of every foll 6th row on all sizes until there are 53 [55:57:59:61] sts. Cont straight until sleeve measures 17 [17½:17¾:18:18½]in (43 [44:45:46:47] cm); end with P row.
Shape top

Bind off 2 sts at beg of next 2 rows.
Next row K1, K2 tog, K to last 3 sts, K2 tog tbl, K1.
Next row P to end.
Rep last 2 rows 3 times more. 41 [43:45:47:49] sts. Cut off yarn and leave sts.

Yoke
Using No. 6 (4½mm) circular needle, A and with RS facing, beg at back and K across all sts on holders, K2 tog at each seam, then K to center back and start all rounds from here. 192 [208:224:240:256] sts. K0 [1:2:3:4] rounds, then cont in stockinette st and patt as foll:
1st round *1 A, 1 D, rep from * to end.
2nd round Work in D.
3rd round *1 D, 1 A, rep from * to end.
4th-5th rounds Work in A.
6th-9th rounds Work from chart A.
10th round Work in A.
11th round Using A, *K6, K2 tog, rep from * to end. 168 [182:196:210:224] sts.
12th-14th rounds As first-3rd rounds, using C instead of D.
15th-16th rounds Work in A.

17th-27th rounds Work from chart B.
28th round Work in A.
29th round Using A, *K5, K2 tog, rep from * to end. 144 [156:168:180:192] sts.
30th-33rd rounds As first-3rd rounds.
34th round Work in A.
35th round Using A, *K4, K2 tog, rep from * to end. 120 [130:140:150:160] sts.
36th-44th rounds Work from chart C.
45th round Work in A.
46th round Using A, *K3, K2 tog, rep from * to end. 96 [104:112:120:128] sts.
47th-49th rounds As 12th-14th rounds.
50th round Work in A.
51st round Using A, *K2, K2 tog, rep from * to end. 72 [75:78:81:84] sts.
Change to four No. 4 (3¾mm) needles. Cont in K2, P2 ribbing, dec 0 [3:2:1:0] sts in 1st round. 72 [72:76:80:84] sts. Work 2½in (6cm) for crew neck or 6 [6:6½:6½:7½]in (15 [15:17:17:19]cm) for turtleneck. Bind off loosely in ribbing.

To finish
Press or block, according to yarn used. Join and press seams.

Shoestring

Coin purse

Make an extra scrap of velvet into a pretty purse.

Finished size
About 4in (10cm) square.

Materials
*Piece of patterned velvet 9×7in
(24×18cm)
Piece of hard-wearing lining fabric
9×7in (24×18cm)
One bag clasp opening 4×1½in
(10×4cm)
Matching thread
Pair of pliers or small hammer
Piece of spare fabric*

1 Cut the velvet in half widthwise into two pieces, each 4½ × 7in (12 × 18cm).
2 Round off the corners on the two pieces. Fold one piece in half lengthwise, then in half again widthwise, and pin folds together. Curve the corners. Open out the piece, and use it as a pattern to round off the corners on the other piece of velvet.
3 Repeat steps 1 and 2 with the piece of lining fabric.
4 On the wrong side of one velvet piece mark a point about 1½in (4cm) down one short side from one long edge. Repeat on opposite short side of the velvet.
5 Place both velvet pieces together with right sides facing and edges matching. Pin, baste and stitch from mark down short edge, across the base and up to second mark, taking ¼in (5mm) seam allowance. At the beginning and end of the stitching, reinforce the ends with a few backstitches.
6 Trim seam and clip in toward the line of stitching at both marks. Turn velvet bag right side out.
7 Repeat steps 4 and 6 with lining pieces, but do not turn lining bag right side out.
8 Place lining bag inside velvet bag with wrong sides together and open edges matching. Pin, baste and zig-zag stitch the two pieces together around the open edges.
9 Push the zig-zag stitched edges into the open channels of the bag clasp very carefully, gathering up the fabric to fit the length of the clasp.
10 Working from the inside of the purse and using pliers or a hammer, firmly squeeze the channels closed to secure the fabric in the clasp. Use a spare piece of material between the clasp and pliers to prevent the clasp from being marked.

*Picking up stitches for a collar
*Knitting a separate collar
*Working a neckband and collar
*Patterns for a child's cardigan and pullover

Picking up stitches for a collar

When picking up and knitting a collar, you should shape the collar so that it sits evenly around the neck without pulling the garment out of shape. There are several ways of doing this.

The first method shown here involves shaping the collar by working a multiple increase row $\frac{1}{2}$in (1.2cm) from the beginning of the collar. The number of stitches should be increased by approximately one-third. The increase should be worked at regular intervals across the row to produce an even shape. When increasing in this way, you can achieve a neater look by using the invisible increase "make 1" method (see Volume 6, page 53).

The second method shows increases worked at each end of every alternate row; this will shape the sides of the collar so that all the corners sit at the front and do not point toward the back.

The third method shows increases worked within several rows so that a decorative collar is formed.

1 First, measure neck of garment: the neck of the garment in our sample measures 17$\frac{3}{4}$in (45cm). Next, knit a gauge swatch using yarn, needles and stitch chosen for collar—here it is K1, P1 ribbing. Calculate gauge for collar to see how many stitches are required.

2 With the wrong side of the work facing, pick up and knit the required number of stitches evenly around neck (this should be an odd number of stitches to balance the ribbing) and work in K1, P1 ribbing for $\frac{1}{2}$in (1.2cm).

3 Increase the stitches across the next row, then continue knitting for the depth required. Bind off loosely: when the collar is turned to the right side and folded back it sits evenly around the neck.

4 Remember that the right side of the collar is knitted in on the WS of the garment—this is especially necessary when working a collar in stockinette stitch or reverse stockinette stitch. Here is a collar knitted in stockinette stitch with 2 stitches worked in garter stitch at each end. A garter stitch border, worked before binding off, prevents the edges from curling.

5 The increases have been worked at each end of this collar. The first increase is worked on the second row and then an increase is worked on every following alternate row, instead of evenly across the row, by working K2, M1, work to within last 2 stitches, M1, K2. On the return rows the 2 border stitches at each end can be either knitted or purled, depending on the effect desired; here they have been purled.

6 This collar has been worked in wide ribbing with invisible increases at each side of the knit ribs on every 4th row.

Knitting a separate collar

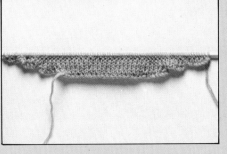

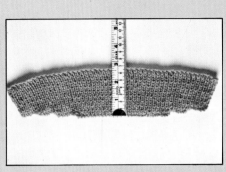

1 Work as step 1 of Picking up stitches for a collar. To produce a collar that will sit neatly all around the neck, you should shape the collar. After calculating the gauge for the collar, cast on the number of stitches equal to the width of the back neck of the garment (this should be an odd number of stitches to balance the ribbing).

2 To build up a gradual shape, cast on groups of stitches (equal to approximately 1in [or 2.5cm]) at the beginning of each row until the collar is the required width. Make sure that the same number of cast-on groups have been worked at each end.

3 Continue knitting until the collar is the required depth (measured at center of collar), then bind off *loosely*.

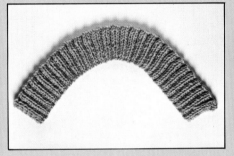

4 With right side of collar to wrong side of neck, sew cast-on edge of collar around neck, then fold collar to right side. Notice how the cast-on groups have shaped the collar so that the side edges lie flat and do not dip toward the front or back neck.

5 The total width of this collar has been cast on and the collar knitted in K2, P2 ribbing.

6 When the collar is sewn around the neck of the garment it tends to sit toward the front. If you want the collar to sit toward the back, cast on fewer stitches and sew it evenly in place.

Working a neckband and collar

1 When working a sweater with a V neckline, you can add a collar very simply as an extension to the neckband. Join the shoulder seams, then, using a set of four needles and following pattern instructions, pick up and knit the neckband, but do not bind off.

2 Now rib the stitches of the back neck and then rib for 2¼in (6cm) along first side of neck. Bind off stitches until there are the same number of stitches left as those knitted on first side of the neck.

3 Rib remaining stitches. Transfer stitches onto one needle, then continue in ribbing for depth of collar required. Bind off loosely in ribbing. The finished sample shows the effect of a neckband and collar combined.

Frederick Mancini

Child's cardigan and pullover

Choose a tweedy yarn to knit these children's sweaters. Both the pullover and the cardigan are knitted in fisherman's rib, making them very warm and cozy to wear.

Sizes
To fit 22[24:26:28]in (56[61:66:71] cm) chest.
Length, 15¼[16¾:18:19½]in (39[43:46:50]cm).
Sleeve seam, 10½[12¼:13½:15]in (27 [31:34:38]cm).
Note Directions for larger sizes are in brackets []; if there is only one set of figures it applies to all sizes.

Materials
Cardigan *10[10:12:12]oz (250: 300:300]g) of a sport yarn in main color (A)*
4[4:4:6[oz (100[100:100:150]g) in contrasting color (B)
Pullover *10[10:12:12]oz (250[250: 300:300]g) of a sport yarn in main color (A)*
2[4:4:4[oz (50[100:100:100]g) in contrasting color (B)
1 pair each Nos. 3 and 6 (3¼ and 4½mm) knitting needles
5 buttons for cardigan
2 buttons for sweater

Gauge
18 sts and 40 rows to 4in (10cm) over patt on No. 6 (4½mm) needles.

Cardigan

Left front
**Using No. 3 (3¼mm) needles and B, cast on 28[30:32:34] sts.
1st ribbing row P1[2:1:2], K2, *P2, K2, rep from * to last 1[2:1:2] sts, P to end.
2nd ribbing row K1[2:1:2], P2, *K2, P2, rep from * to last 1[2:1:2] sts, K to end.
Rep these 2 rows for 2¾[2¾:3:3]in (7 [7:8:8]cm); end with a 2nd row and dec one st at center of last row. 27[29:31:33] sts. Cut off B. Join on A. Change to No. 6 (4½mm) needles. K1 row. Beg patt.
1st row (WS) K2, *K next st inserting needle into st one row below—called knit one below or K1b—, K1, rep from * to last st, K1.
2nd row K1, *K1 b, K1, rep from * to end.
These 2 rows form patt.
Patt 3[3:5:5] more rows.**
Divide for pocket
Next row Patt 10[10:12:12], turn and cast on 11[11:13:13] sts for pocket lining, leave rem sts on a spare needle. Knitting cast-on sts in first row, work 35[35:41:41] rows on these 21[21: 25:25] sts; end with a WS row.
Next row Patt 10[10:12:12], bind off

rem sts. Cut off yarn and leave sts on a spare needle.
Rejoin yarn to first set of sts on spare needle and patt 37[37:43:43] rows; end with a RS row.
Next row Patt to end, then patt across the sts on spare needle.
Cont in patt until work measures 13½[15:16¼:17¾]in (34[38:41:45]cm); end with a WS row.
Shape neck
Next row Patt to last 2 sts, bind off these 2 sts. Cut off yarn.
Turn and rejoin yarn at neck edge. Dec one st at neck edge on next and every foll alternate row until 20[22:23:25] sts rem; end at side edge.
Shape shoulder
Bind off 4[5:4:5] sts at beg of next row and 4[4:5:5] sts at beg of foll 3 alternate rows. Work 1 row. Bind off.

Right front
Work as left front from ** to **.
Divide for pocket
Next row Patt 17[19:19:21], turn and leave rem sts on a spare needle.
Work 36[36:42:42] rows on these sts; end with a RS row. Cut off yarn and leave sts on a spare needle.
Cast on 11[11:13:13] sts for pocket lining, then onto same needle patt the first set of sts on spare needle. Knitting cast-on sts in first row, work 35[35:41: 41] rows on these 21[21:25:25] sts; end with a WS row.
Next row Bind off 11[11:13:13], patt to end.
Next row Patt to end, then patt across the sts on spare needle.
Cont in patt until work measures 13½[15:16¼:17¾]in (34[38:41:45]cm); end with a WS row.
Shape neck
Next row Bind off 2, patt to end.
Complete to match left front.

Back
Using No. 3 (3¼mm) needles and B, cast on 60[64:68:72] sts.
1st ribbing row P1, K2, *P2, K2, rep from * to last st, P1.
2nd ribbing row K1, P2, *K2, P2, rep from * to last st, K1.
Rep these 2 rows for 2¾[2¾:3:3]in (7 [7:8:8]cm); end with a 2nd row and dec one st at center of last row. 59[63:67:71] sts.
Cut off B. Join on A. Change to No.6 (4½mm) needles. K1 row. Cont in patt as

for left front until work measures same as fronts to beg of shoulder; end with a WS row.
Shape shoulders
Bind off 4[5:4:5] sts at beg of next 2 rows, 4[4:5:5] sts at beg of next 6 rows and 4[5:4:5] sts at beg of foll 2 rows. Bind off.

Sleeves
Using No. 3 (3¼mm) needles and B, cast on 38[38:40:40] sts.
1st ribbing row P2[2:1:1], K2, *P2, K2, rep from * to last 2[2:1:1] sts, P to end.

2nd ribbing row K2[2:1:1] P2, *K2, P2, rep from * to last 2[2:1:1] sts, K to end. Rep these 2 rows for 2½[2½:2¾:2¾]in (6[6:7:7]cm); end with a 2nd row and inc one st at center of last row. 39[39:41:41] sts. Cut off B, join on A. Change to No. 6 (4½mm) needles. K1 row. Cont in patt as for left front, inc one st at each end of 12th and every foll 18th[14th:15th:13th] row until there are 47[51:53:57] sts. Cont straight until work measures 10½[12¼:13½:15]in (27[31:34:38]cm); end with a WS row. Bind off loosely.

Collar

Using No. 3 (3¼mm) needles and B, cast on 106[106:110:110] sts.
1st row *P2, K2, rep from * to last 2 sts, P2.
2nd row *K2, P2, rep from * to last 2 sts, K2. Rep these 2 rows for 3¼[3¼:3½:3½]in (8[8:9:9]cm); end with a 2nd row. Bind off loosely in ribbing.

Buttonhole border

Using No. 3 (3¼mm) needles and B, cast on 112[124:136:148] sts.
Ribbing row *K2, P2, rep from * to end.

Rep this row 4 times more.
1st buttonhole row Rib 4, *bind off 2, rib until there are 14[16:18:20] sts on right-hand needle after bound-off group, rep from * 3 times more, bind off 2, rib to end.
2nd buttonhole row Rib to end casting on 2 sts over those bound off in previous row. Rib 5 more rows. Bind off in ribbing.

Button border

Using No. 3 (3¼mm) needles and B, cast on 112[124:136:148] sts.
Ribbing row *P2, K2, rep from * to end. Rep

this row 11 times more. Bind off in ribbing.

Pocket borders (make 2)
Using No. 3 (3¼mm) needles and B, cast on 26[26:30:30] sts.
1st row *P2, K2, rep from * to last 2 sts, P2.
2nd row *K2, P2, rep from * to last 2 sts, K2.
Rep these 2 rows 3 times more. Bind off in ribbing.

To finish
Join shoulder seams. Mark armholes 5¼[5½:5¾:6¼]in (13[14:15:16]cm) from shoulder seams on back and fronts. Sew sleeves to armholes between markers. Join side and sleeve seams. Sew down pocket linings. Sew on pocket borders. Sew cast-on edge of collar to neck edge. Sew borders to front and collar edges, reversing seam for ¾in (2cm) below neck shaping to bound-off edge of collar. Press seams lightly. Sew on buttons.

Pullover

Front
Using No. 3 (3¼mm) needles and B cast on 60[64:68:72] sts. Work 2 ribbing rows of back of cardigan for 2¾[2¾:3:3]in (7[7:8:8]cm); end with a 2nd row and dec one st at center of last row. 59[63:67:71] sts
Cut off B, Join on A. Change to No. 6 (4½mm) needles. K1 row. Cont in patt as for left front work 5[5:7:7] rows.

Divide for pockets
Next row Patt 10[10:12:12], turn and cast on 11[11:13:13] sts for first pocket lining, leave rem sts on a spare needle. Knitting cast-on sts in first row, work

35[35:41:41] rows on these 21[21:25:25] sts; end with a WS row.
Next row Patt 10[10:12:12], bind off rem sts. Cut off yarn and leave rem sts on a spare needle.
Rejoin yarn to first set of sts on spare needle.
Next row Patt 39[43:43:47] sts, turn and leave rem sts on a spare needle. Work 36[36:42:42] rows on these sts; end with a RS row. Cut off yarn and leave sts on a spare needle. Cast on 11[11:13:13] sts onto free needle for 2nd pocket lining, then onto same needle patt across rem sts.
Knitting cast-on sts in first row, work 35[35:41:41] rows; end with a WS row.
Next row Bind off 11[11:13:13] sts, patt to end.
Next row Patt to end, then patt across sts on spare needles.
Cont in patt until work measures 9¼[10¼:11:12]in (23[26:28:30]cm); end with a RS row.

Divide for front opening
Next row Patt 27[29:31:33], bind off 5, patt to end.
Cont on last set of sts until opening edge measures 4¼[4¾:5¼:5¾]in (11[12:13:15]cm); end with a WS row. Shape neck and complete as for left front of cardigan. Rejoin yarn to inner end of rem sts and work until opening edge measures same as other edge; end with a WS row. Shape neck and complete as for right front of cardigan.

Back and Sleeves
Work as back and sleeves of cardigan.

Pocket borders (make 2)
Work as pocket borders of cardigan.

Collar
Using No. 3 (3¼mm) needles and B, cast on 136[136:140:140] sts.
1st row K3, P2, *K2, P2, rep from * to last 3 sts, K3.
2nd row P3, K2, *P2, K2, rep from * to last 3 sts, P3.
Rep these 2 rows for 3¼[3¼:3½:3½]in (8[8:9:9]cm); end with a 2nd row for a boy's sweater or with a first row for a girl's sweater.
Next row Rib 15, bind off 106[106:110:110] sts, rib to end.
Cont on last set of 15 sts, work 6[6:8:8] rows.
Dec one st at beg of next row.
Work 4[6:6:8] rows.
Make a buttonhole over next 2 rows by binding off 2 center sts in the first row and casting on 2 sts over those bound off on foll row.
Work 10[12:14:16] rows.
Make another buttonhole over next 2 rows. Work 8 rows. Bind off firmly in ribbing.
With RS of work facing, rejoin yarn to rem sts.
Work 6[6:8:8] rows.
Dec one st at end of next row.
Work 26[30:32:36] rows.
Bind off firmly in ribbing.

To finish
Join shoulder seams. Mark depth of armholes 5¼[5½:5¾:6¼]in (13[14:15:16]cm) from shoulder seams on back and front. Sew sleeves to armholes between markers. Join side and sleeve seams. Sew down pocket linings. Sew on pocket borders. Sew collar and front borders to neck and front opening. Press seams lightly. Sew on buttons.

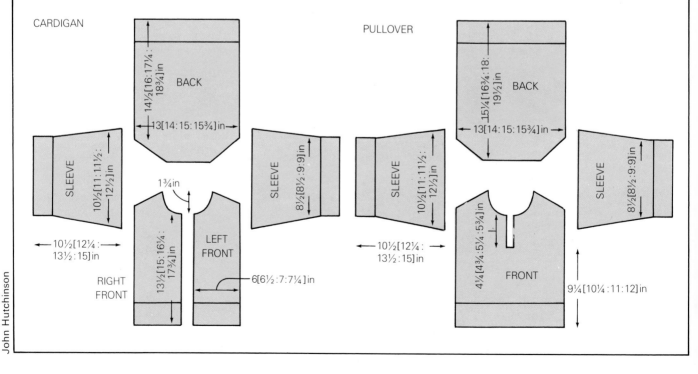

Working collars for square necklines

A shawl collar gives a snug finish to a V neckline and is most frequently seen on jackets and vests (see the vest on page 57). This type of collar is usually worked separately after the garment has been completed. Often it starts at a point from the beginning of the front neck shaping and widens to fit around the back neck: in this way it resembles both a collar and a lapel, but without any indentations.

A shawl collar can also be used to trim a square neckline; crossed at the front, it lies close to the neck and is very warm. Another finish for a square neckline is a sailor collar. This echoes the square shape of the neckline and falls back on the garment away from the neck.

Making a shawl collar

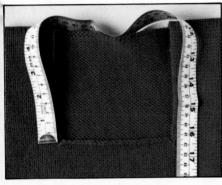

1 To add a shawl collar to a garment that has a square neck at the front, first measure the sides and back neck of the garment. Our sample measures 16in (41cm).

2 Using the chosen yarn, needles and stitch, knit a stitch gauge sample—here it is K1, P1 ribbing. Calculate the gauge and cast on the number of stitches required (this should be an odd number to balance the ribbing).

3 Work in K1, P1 ribbing until the depth of the collar measures the same as the width of the front neck, then bind off loosely in ribbing.

4 Sew cast-on edge of collar around neck, sewing sides (row ends) of collar to front neck, lapping right-hand side over left-hand side for a woman's sweater and vice versa for a man's sweater. Turn back collar to form shawl effect as shown.

5 To work this shawl collar, cast on the stitches required for the width of the collar and then work in garter stitch until collar, when slightly stretched, fits up one side of neck, across back neck and down other side of neck. Sew cast-on and bound-off edges to front neck, overlapping collar as before, then sew collar all around neck. Turn back collar to form shawl as shown.

6 In some cases, particularly on jackets, shaping is worked for the back neck of the collar to produce a good shape. The shaping is formed by working short (or turning) rows to build up the back of the collar—the collar of the vest on page 57 is worked in this way.

Frederick Mancini

Working a sailor collar

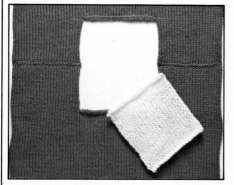

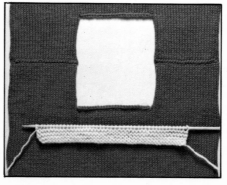

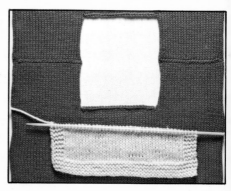

1 To add a collar to a garment that has a square neck at the front and back, first decide on the width of the collar. Using the chosen yarn, needles and stitch, knit a gauge sample. Calculate the gauge and cast on the number of stitches required for the width of the collar.

2 For this type of collar you will need to work a border all around to prevent the edges from curling (unless the collar is worked in ribbing). For our sample we have chosen stockinette stitch with a garter stitch border. Work in garter stitch for ¾in (2cm).

3 Next row (RS) Knit to end. Next row Knit for ¾in (2cm) for side border, purl to last ¾in (2cm), knit to end for other side border. Repeat these 2 rows until the collar measures ¾in (2cm) less than depth to front neck, ending with a RS row.

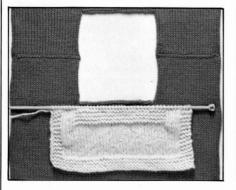

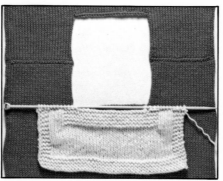

4 On the next row the garter stitch border is introduced for the front neck. To calculate how many stitches you need, measure front neck of garment then add 1½in (4cm) to allow for border to be worked along each side of front neck. Continue in stockinette stitch with center and side borders for a further ¾in (2cm), ending with a RS row.

5 On the next row work to the position of the front neck stitches—the stitches within the garter stitch borders of side neck—bind off front neck stitches, then work to end of row.

6 Continue the garter stitch borders at each end, work on the first group of stitches until inner edge fits along side of neck, ending with a RS row. Cut off yarn and leave this group of stitches on a spare needle.

7 With RS of the work facing, rejoin yarn to inner end of remaining stitches and work to match first side, ending with a WS row.

8 On this row the group of stitches for the back neck are cast on—these should be the same number as those bound off on the front. Cast on stitches then turn and work across the stitches on the spare needle.

9 Complete to match first half of collar, working back neck border for ¾in (2cm). Sew inner edge of collar all around neck, then turn collar to right side.

Vest with shawl collar

This buttoned vest will add a bit of style to a blouse and skirt;
it looks great with slacks, too.

Kim Sayer

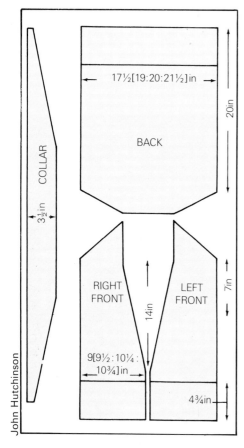

17½[19:20:21½]in

20in

BACK

COLLAR

3½in

RIGHT FRONT

LEFT FRONT

14in

7in

9[9½:10¼: 10¾]in

4¾in

John Hutchinson

Sizes
To fit 32[34:36:38]in (83[87:92:97]cm) bust.
Length, 20in (51cm).
Note: Directions for larger sizes are in brackets []; if there is only one set of figures it applies to all sizes.

Materials
8[9:9:10]oz (200[225:225:250]g) of a sport yarn
1 pair each Nos. 2 and 3 (2¾ and 3¼mm) knitting needles
No. 2 (2¾mm) circular knitting needle 36in (100cm) long
4 buttons

Gauge
30 sts and 36 rows to 4in (10cm) in patt worked on No. 3 (3¼mm) needles.

Back
Using No. 2 (2¾mm) needles cast on 93[100:107:114] sts.
1st row K2, *P2, K1, P2, K2, rep from*.
2nd row P2, *K2, K1, K2, P2, rep from*.
Rep these 2 rows for 4¾in (12cm); end with a first row. Change to No. 3 (3¼mm) needles.
Next row K3, *pick up loop lying between needles and K tbl—called M1—, K3, (M1, K2) twice, rep from * to last 6 sts, (M1, K3) twice. 131[141:151:161] sts. Beg patt.
1st row (RS) K2, *P3, K1, P3, K3, rep from * to last 9 sts, P3, K1, P3, K2.
2nd row P2, *K3, P1, K3, P3, rep from

* to last 9 sts, P3, K1, P3, K2.
3rd row As first row.
4th row K to end.
Rep these 4 rows until work measures 20in (51cm); end with a WS row.
Shape shoulders
Bind off 5 sts at beg of next 14[16:16:18] rows, then 5[4:8:7] sts at beg of foll 2 rows. Bind off rem 51[53:55:57] sts.

Left front
Using No. 2 (2¾mm) needles cast on 48[51:55:58] sts.
1st row K2, *P2, K1, P2, K2, rep from * to last 4[0:4:0] sts, P2, K1, P1[P0:P2, K1, P1:P0].
2nd row K1, P1, K2[K0:K1, P1, K2:K0], P2, *K2, P1, K2, P2, rep from * to end.
Rep these 2 rows for 4¾in (12cm); end with a first row. Change to No. 3 (3¼mm) needles.
Next row K3, (M1, K2) twice [K3:K3, (M1, K2) twice:K3], *M1, K3, (M1, K2) twice, rep from * to last 6 sts, (M1, K3) twice. 67[71:77:81] sts. Beg patt.
1st row (RS) K2, *P3, K1, P3, K3, rep from * to last 5[9:5:9] sts, P3, K1 then P1[P3, K2:P1:P3, K2].
2nd row K1[P2, K3:K1:P2, K3], P1, K3, *P3, K3, P1, K3, rep from * to last 2 sts, P2.
3rd row As first row.
4th row K to end.
Rep these 4 rows once more, then work the first 2 rows again.
Shape front edge
Working in patt, dec one st at end of next and every foll 4th row until 50[54:55:59] sts rem, then at end of every foll 6th row until 40[44:48:52] sts rem. Cont straight until front measures same as back to shoulder; end with WS row.
Shape shoulder
Bind off 5 sts at beg of next and foll 6[7:7:8] alternate rows. Work 1 row. Bind off rem 5[4:8:7] sts.

Right front
Using No. 2 (2¾mm) needles cast on 48[51:55:58] sts.
1st row P1, K1, P2[P0:P1, K1, P2:P0], K2, *P2, K1, P2, K2, rep from * to end.
2nd row P2, *K2, P1, K2, P2, rep from * to last 4[0:4:0] sts, K2, P1, K1[K0:K2, P1, K1:K0].
Rep these 2 rows for 4¾in (12cm); end with a first row. Change to No. 3 (3¼mm) needles.
Next row K3, *M1, K3, (M1, K2) twice, rep from * to last 3[6:3:6] sts, (M1, K3) once [twice:once:twice]. 67[71:77:81] sts.
Beg patt.
1st row (RS) P1 [K2, P3:P1:K2, P3], K1, P3, *K3, P3, K1, P3, rep from * to last 2 sts, K2.
2nd row P2, *K3, P1, K3, P3, rep from *to last 5[9:5:9] sts, K3, P1 then K1[K3, P2:K1:K3, P2].

3rd row As first row.
4th row K to end.
Cont to match left front, reversing all shaping.

Armhole borders
Join shoulder seams. Mark depth of armholes 7in (18cm) from shoulders on back and fronts. Using No. 2 (2¾mm) needles and with RS facing, pick up and K 128 sts along armhole between markers.
Next row P2, *K2, P1, K2, P2, rep from * to end.
Work 1¾in (4cm) ribbing as set. Bind off loosely in ribbing.

Collar
Using No. 2 (2¾mm) circular needle cast on 366 sts. Work 4 rows ribbing as for back waistband.
Next 2 rows Rib to last 7 sts, turn.
Next 2 rows Rib to last 14 sts, turn.
Cont to work 7 sts less on next and every alternate row 7 times more (i.e. 63 sts unworked at each end). Cont across all sts until center back measures 3½in (9cm) from beg. Bind off loosely in ribbing.

To finish
Press or block according to yarn used. Do not flatten patt. Join side seams. Sew cast-on edge of collar to vest, beg and end at top of waistband. Press seams. Sew 4 buttons to left front edge of waistband and make 4 loops on opposite edge.

Keep those loose recipes together in this smart vinyl-covered holder. Hang it on the kitchen wall and it's always close at hand

Handy recipes

Belinda

Finished size
12 × 9½in (30 × 24cm).

Materials
Piece of patterned vinyl, 31½ x 12in (80 x 30cm)
Piece of harmonizing solid-color fabric 31½ x 24in (80 x 60cm)
Two pieces of thin cardboard about 10¾ x 8¾in (27.5 x 22.5cm)
Two 1in (2.5cm) D-rings
Decorative snap fasteners
Matching thread
Transparent tape

1 From vinyl cut two pieces, each 13¼×11in (34×28cm), for back and front and two pieces, each 4¼×2¼in (11×6cm), for hanging loops.
2 From solid-color fabric cut two pieces the same size as the vinyl back and front for the lining. Cut four pieces, each 11×6¼in (28×16cm), for gussets and two pieces, each 8×2¾in (20×7cm), for straps.
3 Turn in ¾in (2cm) on both short edges of each gusset piece. Pin and baste. Place the gusset pieces in pairs, wrong sides facing and edges matching. Pin, baste and topstitch along one finished edge of each pair, ⅜in (1cm) from the edge.
4 Graduate the side edges of the combined gusset pieces from 6¼in (16cm) at topstitched short edge to 1½in (4cm) at lower edge: first mark the centers on lower short edge; mark ¾in (2cm) to each side of bottom center mark. Join these marks to upper corners. Cut along marked lines.
5 Turn ¾in (2cm) to the wrong side on each edge of front. Hold in place with tape. Stitch long edges. Turn in all edges on lining; pin and baste. Place front and lining together with wrong sides facing and edges matching. Fasten with tape.
6 Repeat step 5 with back and lining.
7 Slip one side edge of one gusset piece between edges on one side of front and slip the opposite side of gusset between side edges of back, positioning gusset with wider edge at top and tucking ¾in (2cm) inside front and back pieces. Topstitch down sides, ⅜in (1cm) from edge.
8 Repeat step 7 with remaining gusset on opposite sides of front and back.
9 Place back and front pieces flat, with base edges matching. Topstitch together ⅜in (1cm) from edge, following previous stitching line on vinyl pieces.

10 Fold one strap in half lengthwise. Turn in all edges ⅜in (1cm). Pin, baste and topstitch all around strap ¼in (5mm) from edges.
11 Repeat step 10 to make second strap in the same way.
12 Position straps on each side of back piece, ¾in (2cm) down from the top edge and with ends ¾in (2cm) in from side edges. Sew straps in place by hand, following stitching lines on straps.
13 Fix top half of snap ⅜in (1cm) in on opposite edge of each strap.
14 Fold straps around gusset to front and mark positions of corresponding halves of snaps. Fix corresponding halves of snap to outside front piece to match top halves, first cutting two small squares of lining fabric and placing them underneath the snap positions. Sew on snap.

15 Fix another lower half of a snap to the outside front, between the first snap and each side edge, so that the straps can be extended.
16 Slide one piece of cardboard inside the front, trimming to fit if necessary. Slip stitch front to lining along the top edge.
17 Repeat step 16 with back, but leave edge unstitched.
18 Fold one hanging loop piece in half lengthwise. Turn in long edges for ⅜in (1cm). Pin, baste and topstitch long edges ¼in (5mm) from edge. Thread loop through one D-ring, matching short edges. Repeat to make second loop.
19 Position loops between back and lining pieces 1¼in (3cm) in from side edges. Fasten in place with tape.
20 Slip stitch back to lining, catching each loop in place. Remove the tape.

*Faced seam
*Detachable collar
*Pattern for a jacket with
  peplum (1):
  adapting the pattern

Faced seam

A faced seam is easy to make and gives emphasis to the line of a garment. It can be used on a curved edge such as an armhole seam (see page 62) or on any straight edge. If it is used on a curved edge, the finished seam must not be too wide, because the seam allowances have to be clipped to allow the seam to lie flat. On a straight seam the facing can be as wide as you like.

Straight seam facings do not need to be joined before applying. All facings should be cut to the same shape as the edge to be faced, by the width of the finished seam plus seam allowances. Grain lines should follow the same direction as the grain lines of the garment edge.

If a thick woolen fabric is used for the garment, it is advisable to use a thinner fabric for the facing, such as lightweight wool or lining fabric; this will reduce the bulk of the seam. For added effect, the facing can be a contrasting color.

The following steps show the application of a facing to an armhole where a sleeve is also inserted.

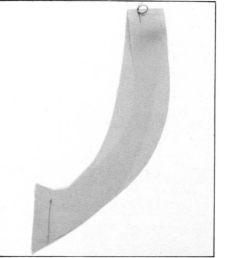

1 With right sides together, baste and stitch the underarm seam of the armhole facing, stitching to within $\frac{1}{4}$in (6mm) of armhole curve and taking a $\frac{5}{8}$in (1.5cm) seam. Press the seam open. Mark the shoulder point with a tailor's tack.

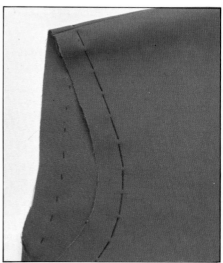

2 After joining the side seam of the garment and pressing the seam open, mark the seamline around the garment armhole with a line of basting stitches.

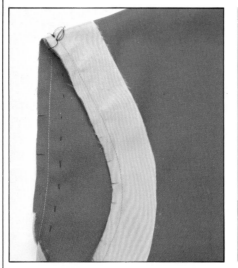

3 With right sides together and matching curved edges, underarm seams and shoulder point, pin, baste and stitch the facing to the armhole edge taking a $\frac{1}{4}$in (6mm) seam. Clip seam allowances almost to the stitching all around. Press.

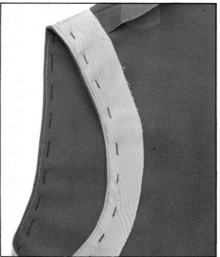

4 Turn facing to the inside and baste in place on the seamline. Press carefully on the curved edge. Topstitch all around $\frac{1}{8}$in (3mm) from the edge.

5 After making the sleeve and pressing the sleeve seam open, insert the sleeve into the armhole, right side of sleeve to right side of facing. Pin it to armhole, matching the underarm seams and shoulder points. Baste the sleeve in place along the seamline.

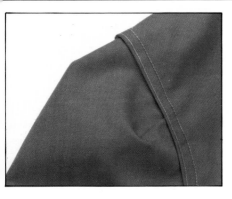

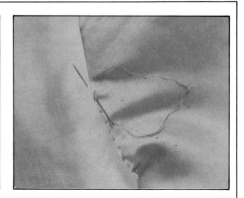

6 Stitch the seam on the seamline. Remove basting and press carefully from the right side using a damp cloth and a dry iron, or a steam iron and dry cloth.

7 If the garment is not lined, finish the armhole seam allowances on the inside of the garment by overcasting them together. Press toward the body.

8 If the garment is lined, the sleeve lining is made with the sleeve and sewn into the garment in one step. The lining is turned in at the armhole edge, brought down over the sleeve and facing, and slip stitched in place over the seamline.

Detachable collar

Besides being decorative, a detachable collar is a practical addition to protect the neck edge of a garment that must be dry cleaned (as on the wool suit on page 62). If you make two collars, you can wear one while the other is in the laundry. Different fashion looks can be obtained by making the collar in different fabrics or shapes. The detachable collar used on the jacket on page 62 echoes the outline of the main collar; it is made of a firm cotton without an interfacing, but if a thin or loosely woven fabric is chosen, it is essential to use an interfacing.

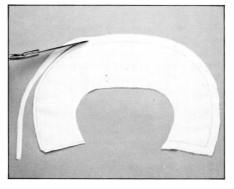

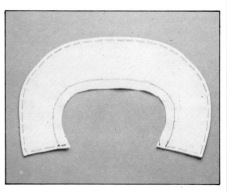

1 With right sides together, baste and stitch the two sections together, taking $\frac{5}{8}$in (1.5cm) seams and leaving the neck edge unstitched. Trim the seam allowance and clip the curved edges almost to the stitching line. Remove basting and press.

2 Turn the collar right side out. Baste around the entire outer edge close to the seam and $\frac{5}{8}$in (1.5cm) from the neck edge. Press.

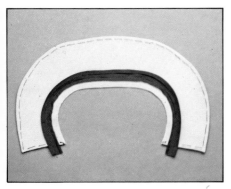

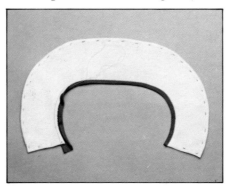

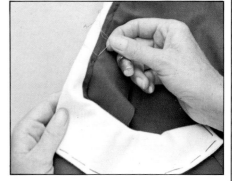

3 Cut a piece of $\frac{1}{2}$in (1.3cm)-wide bias binding to the same measurement as the neck edge, plus $1\frac{1}{4}$in (3cm) for turning in at the ends. Open out one folded edge of the binding; baste and stitch it to the collar on the foldline. The foldline should match the seamline on the neck edge of the collar.

4 Trim the neck edge to $\frac{1}{4}$in (6mm) and clip the curved edge. Press the binding away from the collar, then turn in each end. Turn the binding over the seam allowance and hem to the stitching line, making sure all raw edges are enclosed. Press.

5 Slip stitch the collar to the inside of the neck edge of the garment, matching center backs and fronts. Remove the slip stitching for laundering and replace it later. Alternatively, use small, transparent snap fasteners all around the collar and at matching points on the neck edge of the garment.

Simon Butcher

Jacket with peplum (1)

This jacket with its French styling is a useful addition to your wardrobe. Make it in lightweight wool or cotton. Directions for the matching skirt are given on page 76.

Adapting the pattern

Measurements
The pattern for the jacket is made by adapting the basic dress pattern in the Stitch by Stitch Pattern Pack, available in sizes 10 to 20, corresponding to sizes 8 to 18 in ready-made clothes.

Materials
4 sheets of tracing paper, at least 36 × 40in (90 × 100cm approx)
Yardstick
Right triangle
Flexible curve

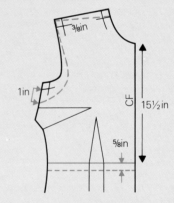

1 For the right front, trace the top half of the dress front pattern. Mark the waistline position by measuring down the center front from the neck cutting line 15½in (39.5cm) for a size 10, adding an extra ¼in (6mm) to this measurement for each larger size.

2 Draw a line across the pattern at this point at a right angle to the center front. This will be the new waistline. Add ⅝in (1.5cm) seam allowance to this edge. Square the shoulder line by raising the shoulder point ⅜in (1cm) and extending it out by ⅜in (1cm). Taper this point into the neck edge seamline.

3 Lower the armhole at the side seam by measuring down from the armhole seamline 1in (2.5cm) and mark. Using a flexible curve, redraw armhole by connecting new shoulder seam to this point.

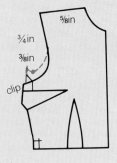

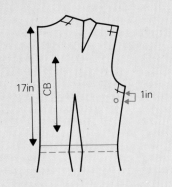

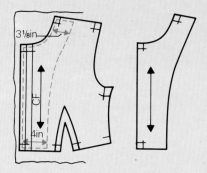

4 Before cutting out pattern, raise armhole seamline by ⅜in (1cm). Re-shape the armhole by folding back the side seam allowance, then tracing this part of the armhole curve. Now open out side seam allowance. Add ¾in (2cm) seam allowance to armhole edge and ⅝in (1.5cm) to shoulder edge. Cut out pattern.

5 The bust dart allowance is transferred to the waist dart: draw a line through the center of the waist dart and extend it 1 in (2.5cm) beyond dart point. Repeat with the bust dart so that the lines cross. Redraw the lower line of the bust dart to meet the intersection of the other lines.

center front edge from the neck edge to the waistline. This allowance is for a button extension and includes a ⅝in (1.5cm) seam allowance. Cut out pattern.

9 To make the back pattern, trace the top half of the dress pattern piece, marking the waist dart. To mark the waistline, measure down the center back seamline from the back neck cutting line 17in (43.5cm) for a size 10, adding an extra ¼in (6mm) to this measurement for each larger size. Square a line across the pattern at this point. Lower armhole at side seam by 1in (2.5cm) and mark.

seam as for the fronts, adding a ¾in (2cm) seam allowance to the armhole edges and a ⅝in (1.5cm) allowance to the shoulders as before. Cut out following the new lines and the center back seamline, noting that this is to be placed on a fold.

13 To make the left front facing pattern, lay tracing paper over the new jacket left front pattern. Trace the shoulder, waistline and front and neck edges.

14 Measure in 3⅛in (8cm) along shoulder seamline from the neck cutting line, and 4in (10cm) in along waistline from front cutting line. Using a flexible curve, and keeping it parallel to the front and neck edges where possible, connect these two points. Mark the seam allowances and cut out.

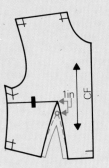

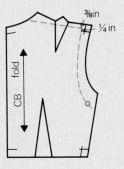

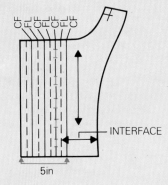

6 Cut along the center line of the waist dart to the intersection. Close the bust dart and tape in place. This will open the pattern at the waist. Re-mark the center point of the waist dart 1in (2.5cm) below the bust point.

7 Add ⅝in (1.5cm) seam allowances to the seamlines of the dart. Mark the grain line on the pattern piece, parallel to the center front. The center front line will be the cutting line. Cut out the pattern.

10 The shoulder dart is removed by taking some of the dart allowance from the armhole edge while the rest is absorbed by the shoulder extension. Measure in along the shoulder seamline from the armhole seamline ¼in (6mm) and up by ⅜in (1cm). Mark, and taper this point into the neck edge seamline.

11 Using a flexible curve, redraw the new armhole curve from the new shoulder point to the mark at the seamline.

15 To make the right fly front and facing, use the right front jacket pattern and follow the directions and measurements given for the left front facing in steps 13 and 14. Add 5in (12cm) extra paper all along front edge for tab fly. Cut out.

16 Within this allowance, mark seven vertical lines at intervals of ⅝in (1.5cm), placing the first line ⅝in (1.5cm) from the center front line and marking it "foldline". Mark the next line "center front" and so on, alternately "foldline" and "center front line". Mark the seam allowances on the facing and mark the grain line parallel to the center front.

17 Mark the vertical buttonholes along the second center front line. The first buttonhole is 1¼in (3cm) from the top cutting line, the remainder spaced at approximately 3¼in (8.5cm) intervals for a size 10 (adjust spacing for larger sizes). Each buttonhole is ⅝in (1.5cm) long, but this measurement can be adjusted.

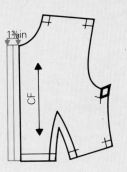

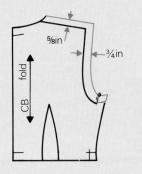

8 To make the left front pattern, turn over the right jacket front pattern piece and trace the shape. Add 1⅜in (3.5cm) to

12 Shape the seam allowance at the side

Brian Mayor

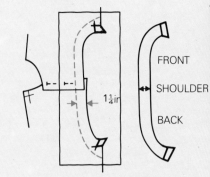

18 To make the armhole facing pattern, overlap the jacket back on one front piece, aligning shoulder seams. Pin or tape down. Trace the front and back armhole cutting lines and the side seam cutting lines. Make the facing 1¼in (3cm) deep all around. Mark the grain line as the shoulder seamline. Mark ⅝in (1.5cm) allowances on side seams. Cut out.

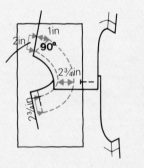

19 To make the back neck facing pattern, lay paper over back pattern, trace the center back and shoulder cutting lines to a depth of 3¼in (8cm) from the neck cutting line. Trace the neck cutting line. The center back is on a fold and will be the grain line.

trace the main collar pattern, making the depth of the collar ⅜in (1cm) less all around. The grain line will be parallel to center back. Mark ⅝in (1.5cm) seamlines and shoulder points and indicate that center back is on a fold.

Sleeve and cuff

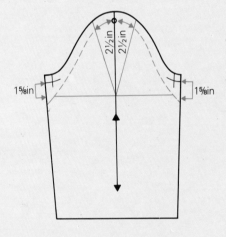

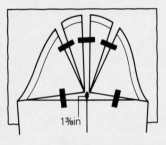

4 Lay sleeve cap over paper, raising intersection point of all lines 1⅜in (3.5cm), spreading top sections evenly for sleeve darts. Tape sleeve in place.

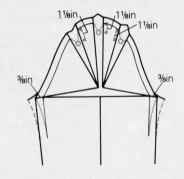

20 To make the collar pattern, lay tracing paper over the front and back neck edges of the jacket (still pinned together at shoulder). Trace the front and back neck seamline and center back seamline, to a depth of 2¾in (7cm) from neck seamline, 2¾in (7cm) depth at shoulder seamline, and 2in (5cm) depth from neck seamline at the center front edge.
21 Using the triangle, measure 1in (2.5cm) from center front edge toward the armhole and mark this point. This is the point of the collar. Using the flexible curve, draw a line joining this point and the other points at shoulder and center back, keeping the line evenly curved all around. Add ⅝in (1.5cm) allowances to all edges except center back, which is placed on a fold.
22 To make the detachable collar pattern,

1 To make the sleeve pattern, trace the basic sleeve pattern, extending the grain line to the top of the sleeve cap. Drop the underarm curve on both sides by 1⅝in (4cm) and mark.
2 Using a flexible curve, redraw the curve from the underarm seam, tapering into the original seamline at the sleeve cap. Draw a line across the pattern at the underarm point at right angles to the grain line.
3 Mark two points on the sleeve cap seamline, each 2½in (6.5cm) from the extended grain line. Connect these points to the intersection of the grain line and horizontal line. Slash along these three lines to the intersection point, and along each part of the horizontal line. This will allow the pattern to be spread.

5 To shape the darts at the sleeve cap, measure along the center of each slash 1⅛in (3cm) from the seamline and mark. Mark dart lines, folding each dart in place with the center and front dart toward the front of the jacket pattern and the back dart toward the back of the pattern. Cut the dart shaping on the cutting line, open out the darts and cut out the rest of the sleeve pattern.
6 Mark ⅝in (1.5cm) seam allowances all around and trace position of the original grain line. Mark a point on the horizontal line ⅜in (1cm) in from cutting line at underarm. Connect this to the underarm seamline. Mark new seam allowance. Repeat with other side.

using the same measurements as before to make the basic peplum shape. Draw a line through the center of the waist dart to the lower edge. Connect a line to each side of the dart from the peplum edge to the waist seamline.

6 Close the dart and tape in place. Add $\frac{5}{8}$in (1.5cm) seam allowances to waist and peplum hem edges. The center back will be placed on a fold and the grain line will be parallel to the center back.

Lining

cutting line for lining

$1\frac{3}{8}$in

outline of facing

1 To make the jacket lining pattern, use the jacket front and back pieces, marking the lining cutting line on each piece. Lay right front fly and facing pattern under jacket right front pattern, matching upper and lower edges. Pin together.

2 Following the curved outer edge of the facing, measure in $1\frac{3}{8}$in (3.5cm) and draw a line parallel to the facing edge from shoulder to waistline. When cutting out the fabric, cut to this line only for the lining for left and right front.

cut lining to here

3 Repeat with the back pattern, laying back pattern under back neck facing and drawing a new cutting line for lining, using measurements as before.

4 Cut the sleeve lining pattern to the same measurements as the sleeves. Transfer all markings to all pieces.

Note: To make the belt pattern, follow directions for making a self-fabric belt in Volume 9, page 61, making the finished width of the belt $1\frac{1}{8}$in (3cm). If a wider belt is needed, allow extra fabric. Directions making the jacket continue on page 68.

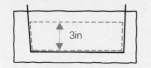

3in

7 To make the cuff pattern, trace the lower edge of the sleeve, making the cuff depth 3in (7.5cm). Divide the cuff into four equal parts.

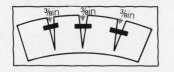

$\frac{3}{8}$in $\frac{3}{8}$in $\frac{3}{8}$in

8 Lay the cuff over tracing paper and slash along each line from the top edge of the cuff to the seamline at wrist edge. Spread each slash $\frac{3}{8}$in (1cm) at the top and tape in place.

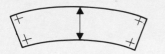

9 Mark $\frac{5}{8}$in (1.5cm) seam allowance around the edges. The grain line runs through the center of the cuff.

Peplum

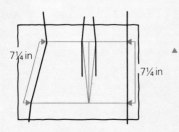

$7\frac{1}{4}$in

$7\frac{1}{4}$in

1 To make the front peplum pattern, use the jacket front pattern to mark the

waistline position on the basic dress front pattern and trace the lower part of the dress: measure from waist seamline down center front line $7\frac{1}{4}$in (18.5cm) for sizes 10 to 14, $7\frac{5}{8}$in (19.5cm) for sizes 16 to 20. Repeat this measurement with side seamline. Draw a horizontal line to connect these two points.

2 Draw a line through the center of the dart from the waistline to the peplum edge. From the peplum edge draw a line up to each side of the dart at the waistline.

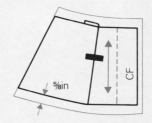

$\frac{5}{8}$in

CF

3 Close the dart and tape in place. Add $\frac{5}{8}$in (1.5cm) seam allowance to waist, center front edge, and peplum hem edge.

4 Cut out the pattern, marking seamline, center front and grain line parallel to the center front line. For the interfacing, trace the center front and upper and lower edges and draw a line parallel to the center front and $1\frac{5}{8}$in (4cm) away from it.

CB fold

$\frac{5}{8}$in

5 To make the back peplum pattern, follow the directions for the front peplum

Brian Mayor

Shoestring

Tasty trimmings

These pins will brighten up any plain top or jacket. Made from scraps of felt they're quick and easy to assemble.

Materials

Scraps of felt in red, green and purple
One small gold-colored safety pin
for each pin
Small green beads for strawberry
Suitable stuffing
Matching thread

Strawberry

Finished size
$3\frac{1}{2} \times 2$in (9×5cm).

1 From red felt cut out two strawberry shapes.
2 Place strawberry shapes together. Pin baste and sew all around, close to the edge, leaving a small opening at the top. Turn right side out. Stuff strawberry firmly; pin opening together to close temporarily.
3 From green felt cut out a strip $1\frac{3}{4} \times \frac{5}{8}$in ($4.5 \times 1.5$cm) for stalk. Roll into a stalk shape from both sides; pin, baste and sew down the center.
4 Fit the stalk into the opening at the top of the strawberry. Sew in place.
5 From green felt cut out one leaf. Cut a small hole in the center of the leaf.
6 Backstitch along each leaf to form veins.
7 Slip the leaf over the stalk and sew it in place on top of the strawberry.
8 Sew tiny green beads all over one side of the strawberry.
9 Sew a safety pin horizontally to the other side of strawberry.

Bunch of grapes

Finished size
4×3in (10×8cm).

1 From purple felt cut out ten ovals about $1\frac{1}{2} \times 1\frac{1}{4}$in ($4 \times 3.5$cm) for grapes.
2 Place the grapes together in pairs; sew them together as for strawberry, step 2.
3 Make four stalks and sew them to four of the five grapes as for strawberry, steps 3 and 4.
4 Make one stalk 3in (8cm) long in the same way and sew it to the top of the remaining grape for the main stem.
5 Place all the short stalks together on top of the long main stalk and sew them in place.
6 From green felt cut out one grape leaf. Backstitch along the leaf to form veins.
7 Sew the leaf to the main stalk over the ends of the smaller stalks.
8 Sew a safety pin vertically to the back of the main stalk.

LEAF
CUT 1 IN GREEN FELT

STRAWBERRY
CUT 2 IN RED FELT

LEAF
CUT1 IN
GREEN FELT

*Tab fly front and facing
*Jacket with peplum (2):
 directions for making

Tab fly front and facing

This technique looks complicated but is in fact very simple and gives a professional touch to a tailored jacket. Here it is finished with a collar at the neck edge and a peplum at the waist, but it is quite easy to adapt to other styles—follow the directions, omitting any parts not needed. The tab fly covers the fastenings and is therefore ideal for raincoats, as it gives added protection against the weather.

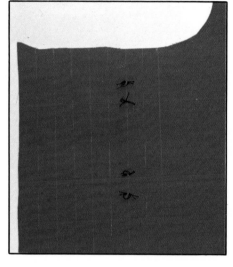

1 Mark the foldlines, center front lines and buttonholes with tailor's tacks or chalk on the right side of the tab fly section.

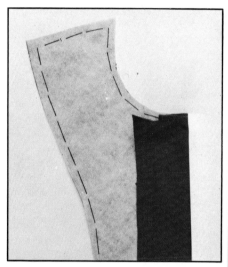

2 Baste interfacing to the wrong side of the tab fly facing and catch-stitch the interfacing to the first foldline from the curved edge. Accordion-pleat the fly piece along the marked foldlines. Press.

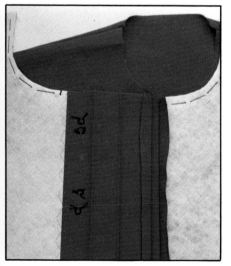

3 With right sides together, baste and stitch the tab fly facing to the right front edge, and the interfaced left facing to the left front edge of the garment. Grade seam allowances and press them toward the facings.

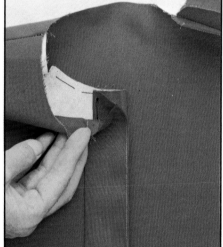

4 Fold the tab fly back in place and turn the fly facing to the inside of the jacket. Baste along the outer folded edge and inner folded edge of the tab fly to hold the pleats in place, keeping the facing free. Topstitch $\frac{1}{4}$in (6mm) in along the outer folded edge through double thickness only.

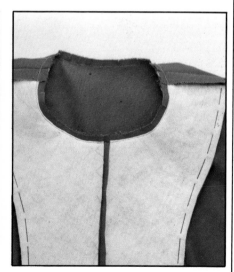

5 Make the collar, baste in place and join back neck to front facing at shoulder seams, following the directions for making. With right sides together, fold the right front facing back over tab fly and collar. Fold left facing back over the collar. Baste all around neck edge and complete as directed on page 70. *continued*

Simon Butcher

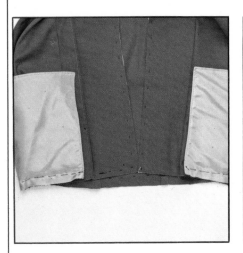
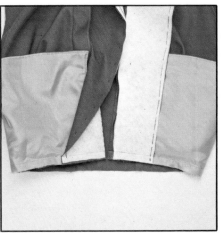

6 Make the peplum section, join the underarm seams of the jacket and baste the peplum to the waistline edge of the jacket, matching notches and following directions for making. Keep the right and left front jacket facings free.

7 Fold the right facing and the left facing back over to the right side of the garment on the foldline of each piece. Baste and stitch around the entire waist edge on the seamline.

8 Clip and grade the seams, press and turn facing to the wrong side of the garment, pressing the seam allowance upward. Topstitch $\frac{1}{4}$in (6mm) away from the inner seamline of the tab fly through all thicknesses. Topstitch along left front, stitching $\frac{1}{4}$in (6mm) in from front edge. Press. Complete with buttonholes.

Jacket with peplum (2)

Here are directions for the jacket begun on page 62.

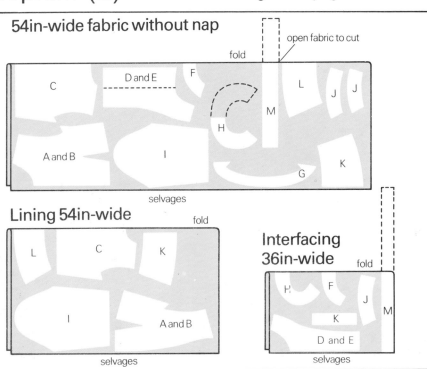

54in-wide fabric without nap
open fabric to cut
fold

C
D and E
F
L
J J
M
H
A and B
I
K
G
selvages

Lining 54in-wide
fold

L
C
K
I
A and B
selvages

Interfacing 36in-wide
fold

H
F
J
K
M
D and E
selvages

Brian Mayor

Directions for making

Suggested fabrics
Light- to medium-weight wool, gabardine, double knits; lining: rayon, polyester or silk surah, moiré or satin. Detachable collar: cotton piqué, linen or satin.

Materials
54in (140cm)-wide fabric without nap:
    Sizes 10, 12: $2\frac{3}{8}$yd (2.1m)
    Sizes 14, 16, 18, 20: $2\frac{1}{2}$yd (2.2m)
54in (140cm)-wide fabric for lining:
    Sizes 10, 12, 14, 16: $1\frac{3}{8}$yd (1.2m)
    Sizes 18, 20: $1\frac{1}{2}$yd (1.3m)
36in (90cm)-wide interfacing:
    for all sizes: $\frac{3}{4}$yd (.7m)
54in (140cm)-wide fabric for detachable contrast collar:
    For all sizes: $\frac{1}{2}$yd (.4m)
12in (30cm) square polyester batting
1$\frac{1}{4}$in (3.2cm)-wide buckle
Five $\frac{1}{2}$in (1.3cm)-diameter buttons
Belt stiffening 1$\frac{1}{4}$in (3cm)-wide:
    $1\frac{1}{8}$yd (1m) for sizes 10-16; $1\frac{1}{4}$yd (1.1m) for sizes 18 to 20
1 pair shoulder pads, matching thread
Bias binding (optional)

Key to adapted pattern pieces

A Jacket right front	Cut 1	
B Jacket left front	Cut 1	
C Jacket back	Cut 1 on fold	
D Left front facing	Cut 1	
E Right fly front and facing	Cut 1	
F Back neck facing	Cut 1 on fold	
G Front and back armhole		

facing	Cut 2
H Collar	Cut 2 on fold
(Detachable collar: Cut 2 on fold from contrasting fabric)	
I Sleeve	Cut 2
J Cuff	Cut 4
K Front peplum	Cut 2
L Back peplum	Cut 1 on fold

M Belt	Cut 1

Lining: use pieces A Cut 1, B Cut 1, C Cut 1 on fold, I Cut 2, K Cut 2, L Cut 1 on fold.
Interfacing: use pieces D Cut 1, E Cut 1, F Cut 1 on fold, H Cut 1 on fold, J Cut 2, K Cut 2 (to facing width only), M Cut to half width only.

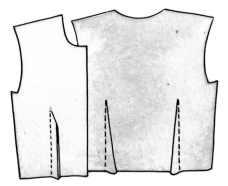

1 With right sides together, fold, baste and stitch the front and back waist darts. Press all darts toward the center.

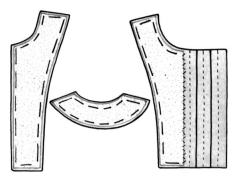

2 Baste the interfacing to the wrong side of the jacket left front facing, jacket back neck facing, and the right tab fly facing. Catch-stitch the interfacing to the foldline of fly.

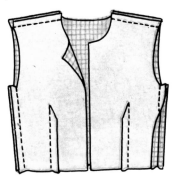

3 With right sides together, baste and stitch the shoulder and side seams of the jacket. Press seams open.

4 Make the right front tab fly and the faced left front section as shown on pages 67-68. Press well.

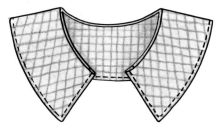

5 Baste the interfacing to the wrong side of one collar section. With right sides together, baste and stitch both collar pieces together, leaving the neck edge open. Trim interfacing close to stitching, trim seam allowance and clip corners. Clip curved outer edges. Press.

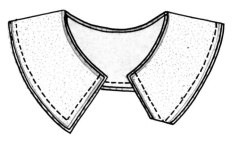

6 Turn the collar right side out and baste around entire outer edge. Press carefully. Topstitch ¼in (6mm) in from the outer edge. Press.

7 With right sides together, matching shoulder points, center fronts and center backs, baste the collar to the neck edge. Do not baste in the facings at this stage.

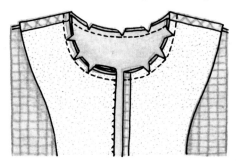

8 With right sides together, join the back neck facing to the front facings, taking ⅝in (1.5cm) seams. Finish the outer edges

of the facing with overcasting. With right sides together, fold back and baste the facings to the neck edge over the collar as shown on page 67. Stitch in place. Grade seams, remove basting, clip curves. Press well.

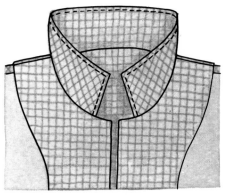

9 Turn the facings to the inside of the jacket and catch-stitch to the shoulder seams. Press well on the seamline only. The lower edge of the front facings are completed after the peplum is attached to the waist.

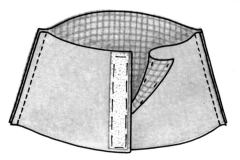

10 Baste the interfacing to the wrong side of the peplum front edge. With right sides together, baste and stitch the front and back peplum pieces at the side seams. Press seams open. Repeat with the peplum lining pieces.

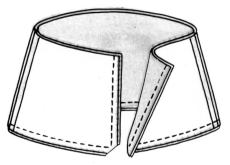

11 With right sides together and seams matching, baste and stitch the lining to the front and hem edges of the peplum. Trim the seam allowances, trimming the interfacing close to the stitching.
12 Turn the peplum right side out. Baste around edges. Press. Topstitch ¼in (6mm) in from front and lower edges. Press.

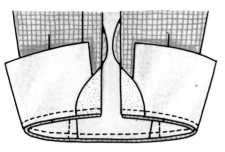

and the sleeve lining. Press seams open. Cut a semi-circle of thin batting to fit the sleeve cap to the dart point, extending down each side to just below the dart shaping. Catch-stitch the batting to the seamline.

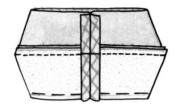

13 With right sides together and matching side seams, center fronts and center backs, baste the peplum to the waistline edge of the jacket.
Fold the facings back over the peplum lining and complete the peplum as shown on page 68.

17 Baste the interfacing to the wrong side of one cuff piece. With right sides together, baste and stitch the two sections together across the top edge. Trim the seam allowances, trimming the interfacing close to the stitching.

19 Turn the cuff right side out and fold it in half along the seamed edge. Baste and press. Topstitch $\frac{1}{4}$in (6mm) in from this edge. Press.

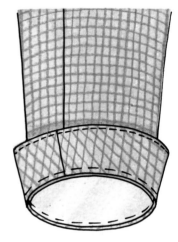

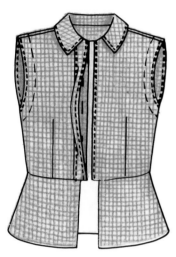

18 Open out the cuff and bring the short edges together, matching center seams. Press the center seam allowance to one side, baste and stitch seam. Trim the interfacing and press the new seam open.

20 With right sides together, and matching sleeve seam to short seam of cuff, baste the cuff to the lower edge of the sleeve, taking a $\frac{5}{8}$in (1.5cm) seam.

14 Turn the facings right side out. Press waist seam allowance up. Topstitch the inner edge of the right tab fly and the left front close to the seamlines as shown on page 68. Make the vertical buttonholes on the lower part of the tab fly and sew corresponding buttons to the left front. Face the jacket armholes as directed on page 60.
15 With right sides together, fold, baste and stitch the sleeve cap darts of the sleeve and sleeve lining. Press darts without marking fabric. The darts in the sleeve lining are pressed in the opposite direction to those in the sleeve.

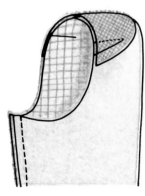

16 With right sides together, baste and stitch the underarm seam of the sleeve

Terry Evans

Chris Harvey

71

21 With right sides together, slip the lining over the sleeve and cuff. Matching seams, baste the lining to the lower edge of the sleeve. Stitch around lower edge, taking a $\frac{5}{8}$in (1.5cm) seam and securing cuff. Trim the seam allowances, trimming the interfacing close to the stitching.

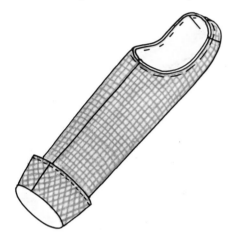

22 Pull the lining down to the lower edge of the sleeve, and slip it inside. Turn the cuff back toward the sleeve and press lower edge. Baste the lining to sleeve around armhole. Repeat steps 15-22 to make the other sleeve and cuff.

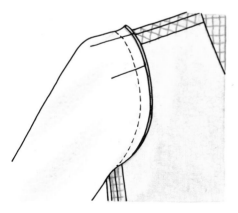

23 Baste the lining to the sleeve at the sleeve cap, covering the sleeve padding, and stitch the sleeve and lining into the jacket armhole as shown on page 61.

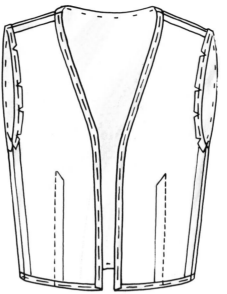

24 With right sides together, baste and stitch the front and back waist darts of the jacket lining, and the shoulder and side seams. Press darts toward center and press seams open. Clip the back neck curve and armhole curves to within $\frac{1}{4}$in (6mm) of the seamline. Turn under the seam allowance around entire neck, hem and armhole edges and baste. Press.

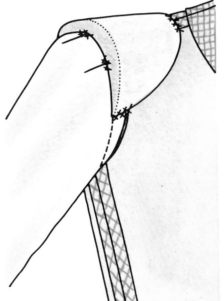

25 Slip stitch the shoulder pads in position at the shoulder on the main garment, making sure that the outer edges of the pads do not project beyond the seamline. Catch-stitch pads to the shoulder seams and shoulder points.
26 With wrong sides together and shoulder and side seams matching, overlap the lining on the outer edge of the neck facings by $\frac{5}{8}$in (1.5cm). Pin the lining to the facing. Pin the lining to the waistline, enclosing the seam allowances at the waist.

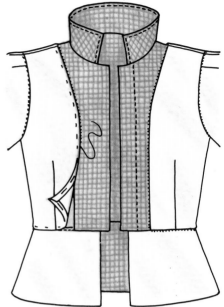

27 Slip stitch the lining to the front and back neck facings, waistline and armhole seamline, enclosing all the raw edges of the seams. Press gently.
28 Make a self-fabric belt as directed in Volume 9, page 61, omitting the overlap allowance if using a clasp-type buckle. Make two fabric belt carriers and attach to side seams centered over the waistline (see Volume 8, page 67).
29 Make the detachable collar from contrasting fabric and attach to the main garment as shown on page 61. This collar is optional and can be omitted if using a tweedy fabric.

*Dior pleat (false pleat)
*Raised seam with pleat
*Pattern for skirt with
  raised seam pleats:
  adapting the pattern;
  directions for making

Dior pleat (false pleat)

This type of pleat gets its name from the designer Christian Dior; it was a popular technique with this fashion house for many seasons. It is in fact a false pleat and is useful because it hangs well when worn, does not take a great deal of fabric and can be made in contrasting color or texture if desired. The Dior pleat on the skirt on page 76 is made in the center back of the skirt. Here we show a method of finishing the skirt pleat and hem edges with overcasting stitches, but if you are using a wool fabric that ravels, it is best to bind these edges and make the underlay with a lining before completing the hem.

1 With right sides together, baste and stitch the center back seam to the top of the pleat position. Finish the seam allowances and outer edge of the pleat and press open.

2 Mark the hemline all along the skirt back and pleat with basting. Part of the back hem allowance is turned up so that the back pleat can be completed: open out the pleat allowance on each side of the skirt back. Turn up the hem allowance, folding along basting. Cut away part of the hem allowance on the pleat section, leaving 1in (2.5cm) hem allowance at bottom of pleat. Finish raw edge of hem.

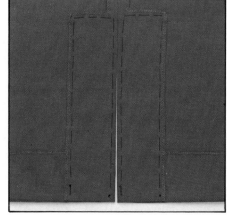

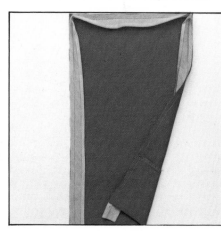

3 Baste along the fold of the hem. Starting at the center back and working toward the side seams, sew the hem to the skirt for approximately 8in (20cm). Use the blind hem method (see Volume 4, page 72). Press folded edge of hem lightly.

4 Turn the pleat back to the inside of the garment. Press folded edge of hem lightly and baste along the folded edges. Press. Slip stitch the pleat to the hem allowance and baste the pleat to the skirt.

5 Turn the pleat underlay hem allowance to the wrong side and baste close to the folded edge. Finish and sew hem in place in the same manner as the skirt. Cut bias binding to fit top and side edges of underlay plus seam allowance at each end. Open out one long edge of the binding and, with right sides together, baste to top and side edges. Stitch binding in place, mitering corners.

continued

Simon Butcher

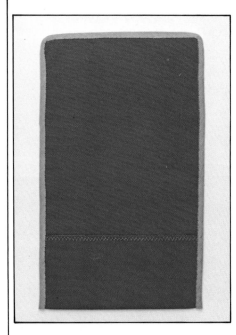

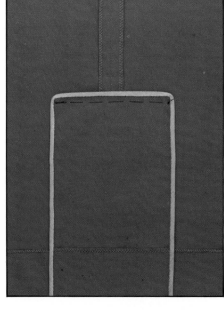

6 Turn in the ends of the binding and fold the binding to the wrong side of the underlay. Slip stitch the binding to the stitching line all around. Press.

7 Lay the skirt back section flat, with the wrong side facing upward. With the right side of the underlay to the wrong side of the skirt, pin the top edge of underlay to the top edge of pleat position. Baste in place along the top edge on the seamline through all thicknesses.

8 Working from the right side of the skirt, stitch underlay in place along the top edge following the basting. Press. The top pleat sections and the hem edge should be held in place by this stitching, but you could add one or two catch-stitches at the center of the pleat length on the inside.

Raised seam with pleat

This method of making a raised seam incorporates a basic knife pleat with a raised tuck effect seam. It coordinates with the raised effect on the faced seam of the jacket on page 69. It gives a decorative finish to a practical technique.

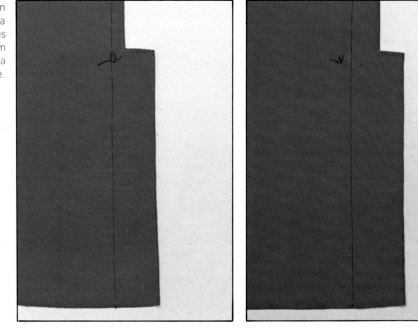

1 Finish the front seam allowances and edges of the pleat. On the front panel mark the foldline of seam and pleat, and top of the pleat position with basting.

2 Finish the side front seam allowances and edges of the pleat. Mark the seamline and pleat line with a row of basting stitches. Mark the top of the pleat position with a tailor's tack.

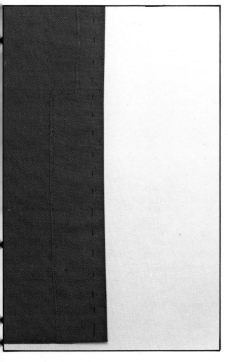

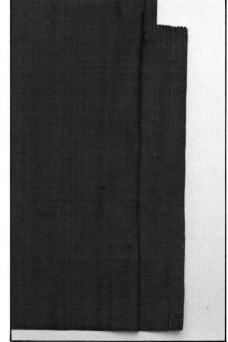

3 On the front panel, fold the seam allowance and pleat to the wrong side along the basting line. Baste in place on the seamline. Press folded edge lightly. Topstitch very close to the edge from top to hem.

4 With the right side of the skirt panels facing upward, lay the front panel over the side panel, matching seamlines and top pleat positions. Pin and baste in place on the seamline.

5 Working from the wrong side of the garment and keeping the front panel free from the stitching, fold the front panel back and baste and stitch the inside edge of the pleat through both thicknesses.

6 Working from the right side, stitch the front panels of the skirt together. Begin the stitching about 1 in (2.5cm) in from the inner end of the pleat, and stitch up to the waist on the seamline.

7 Mark the hemline with basting stitches. Clip the pleat seam almost to the stitching line at the top of the hem. Press the seam open and trim the lower part of the seam allowance to half width. This grading will reduce the thickness when the hem is turned up.

8 Make the rest of the skirt as directed. Finish and turn up the hem edge. Press. Fold the pleat in place and press. Continue the second stitching line (the seamline) down the folded edge to the hem. Baste over fold to hold it in place until skirt is worn.

Simon Butcher

Skirt with raised seam pleats

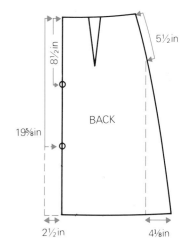

This stylish skirt with pleats teams with the jacket on page 62.

Adapting the pattern

Measurements
The pattern for this skirt is made by adapting the pattern for the basic skirt from the Stitch by Stitch Pattern Pack, available in sizes 10 to 20, which correspond to sizes 8 to 18 in ready-made clothes.

Materials
4 sheets of tracing paper 36×40in (90×100cm)
Yardstick; right triangle
Flexible curve

1 To make the skirt back pattern, trace the basic skirt back pattern, leaving extra paper at the center back. Measure in $4\frac{1}{8}$in (10.5cm) from side cutting line at hem edge and mark this point. Measure down $5\frac{1}{2}$in (14cm) from the waist edge on the side cutting line and mark.

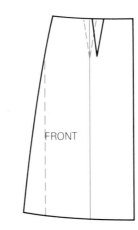

FRONT

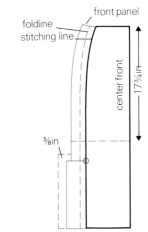

front panel

foldline
stitching line

center front

17¾in

⅝in

2 Using a yardstick, join the two points, curving the line slightly over the hips. The seam allowance has been included along this edge. Measure down 8½in (21.5cm) from waist cutting line on center back line and mark for zipper position.

3 Measure down 19⅝in (50cm) from the waist cutting line on the center back line to mark the point for the top of the pleat opening. Extend the hemline from the center back line 2½in (6.5cm). Draw a line parallel to the center back from this point to the top pleat position.

4 Add ⅝in (1.5cm) seam allowance to the center back edge and top pleat section. Cut out the pattern, marking the seamlines, center back and dart, and the grain line parallel to the center back.

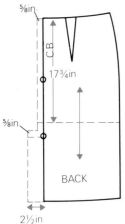

⅝in

C.B.

17¾in

⅝in

BACK

2½in

5 To mark the cutting line for the lining, measure down the center back line from the waist cutting line edge 17¾in (45cm) for sizes 10 to 14; 18½in (47cm) for sizes 16 to 20. Draw a horizontal line across the pattern to the side edge. Use the top half of the pattern for the lining.

6 To make the back pleat underlay, draw a rectangle 12⅝ × 5¾in (32 × 14.5cm) for a size 10, adding an extra ⅜in (1cm) to the longest edge for each larger size.

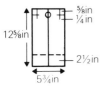

⅝in
¼in

12⅝in

2½in

5¾in

7 Mark the center back line and grain line through the center of the rectangle. Mark a ⅝in (1.5cm) seam allowance at the top edge; ¼in (6mm) along the side edges, and 2½in (6.5cm) at the hem. All these allowances have been included in the underlay measurements.

8 To adjust the front pattern, trace the basic skirt front pattern. Lay the skirt tracing over the new back pattern matching the top side edges of the skirt. Trace the new side edge. Mark the center point between the center front and new side seam at the waist and hem edges.

9 Connect these two points with a yard-stick. Move the waist dart over to this center line by tracing the dart from the pattern and redrawing it with the bisecting line running through the center.

10 To make the front panel pattern, trace the front panel of the new skirt pattern, following the center front line, waist and hem edges. Trace the dart stitching line on this panel only, following the bisecting line down to the hem edge. This line is now the stitching line.

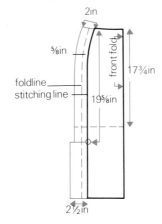

2in

⅝in

front fold

17¾in

foldline
stitching line

19⅝in

2½in

11 Remove the tracing and measure down the stitching line from the waist edge 19⅝in (50cm) on it. Mark a point for the top of the pleat. To this stitching line, add 2in (5cm) seam allowance from the waist cutting line edge to the top of the pleat. Mark the seam and pleat foldline ⅝in (1.5cm) out from the stitching line down the entire length.

12 For the pleat allowance extend the hem edge out from the stitching line 2½in (6.5cm) and mark. Extend a line from the pleat position 2½in (6.5cm) wide and at right angles to the center front. Mark. Connect these two points to make the pleat extension, which will be parallel to the center front.

13 Add ⅝in (1.5cm) allowance all around the pleat extension. Mark the seam and pleat foldline ⅝in (1,5cm) from the stitching line.

14 To make the cutting line for the lining, measure down center front 17¾in (45cm)

for sizes 10 to 16, 18½in (47cm) for sizes 16 to 20, from waist edge. Draw a line across the pattern at this point. Trace and cut out the pattern, marking all seamlines, foldlines and the grain line parallel to the center front. The center front is a fold.

15 To make the side front panel, lay tracing paper over the adapted skirt front pattern, and trace the side panel. Follow the waist, side and hem edges, and the dart stitching line on this panel only, down the bisecting line to the hem edges. Leave extra paper at this edge for the seam allowance and pleat.

16 Mark the grain line parallel to the center front. To mark the top of the pleat, lay the side panel over the front panel, matching stitching lines, waist and hem edges, and trace the top pleat position. For the pleat allowance, extend the top pleat position by 1⅝in (4cm) at right angles to the grain line. Extend the hem edge by the same amount and connect these two points.

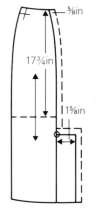

⅝in

17¾in

1⅝in

Brian Mayor

17 Add ⅝in (1.5cm) allowance down the whole of this edge and pleat edge. To mark the lining cutting line, measure down the inner seam edge 17¾in (45cm) for sizes 10 to 14, 18½in (47cm) for the larger sizes, and draw a line across the pattern at this point.

18 To make the waistband pattern, trace the basic waistband and re-mark the notches for the side seam positions. The skirt has a center back zipper opening.

Directions for making

Materials

*54in (140cm)-wide fabric with or
without nap:*
    Sizes 10, 12: 1⅞yd (1.7m)
    Sizes 14-20: 2¼yd (2m)
54in (140cm)-wide lining fabric:
    Sizes 10, 12, 14: 1⅛yd (1m)
    Sizes 16, 18, 20: 1¼yd (1.1m)
36in (90cm)-wide interfacing
    Sizes 10 to 16: 6in (15cm)
    Sizes 18, 20: 10in (25cm)
Matching thread
8in (20cm) skirt zipper
1 card matching bias binding
Hook and eye

Key to adjusted pattern pieces

A Skirt front panel	Cut 1 on fold
B Side front panel	Cut 2
C Back	Cut 2
D Waistband	Cut 1
E Pleat underlay	Cut 1

For the lining: use pieces **A, B, C** cut to
length in pattern adaptation.
For the interfacing: use piece **D** cut to
half width only.

Suggested fabrics

Light- to medium-weight wool—flannel,
gabardine, houndstooth; medium-weight
cotton twill, sailcloth; linen or viscose
slub-weaves. Lining: viscose, polyester
or antistatic nylon.

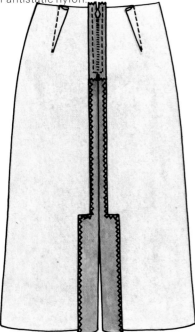

1 With right sides together, fold, baste and
stitch the back waist darts. Press darts
toward center. With right sides together,
baste and stitch the center back seam
leaving an opening for the zipper. Finish
seam and pleat edges. Press the seam
open and insert the zipper into the center
back seam.

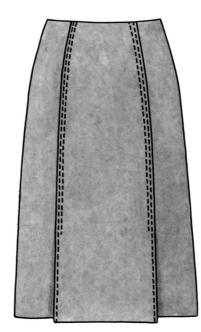

2 Make a Dior pleat into the back seam
as shown on page 73. Turn up the hem
on the **underlay section only.** Sew the
front and side front panels of the skirt
together using the raised seam method
as shown on page 74. Complete each
front pleat as directed, omitting the
final topstitching until the hem is
completed. **Do not** turn up the hem until
the side seams are stitched together.

3 With right sides together, baste and
stitch the side seams. Finish the seam
edges with overcasting and press the
seams open. Turn up the hem all around
and complete it, following directions for
completing hems as shown on page 75.

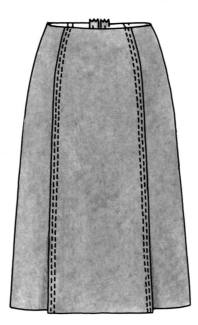

4 Continue the topstitching down to the
hem on the raised seam pleats as
directed on page 75, beginning the
stitching where the stitching finishes on
the seamline.

5 When the back pleat is complete, add
a row of topstitching close to the fold of
the pleat on each side. Begin the stitching
from the hem edge and stitch as far as
possible into the top corner. Leave
enough thread to complete the last
few stitches at the top by hand.

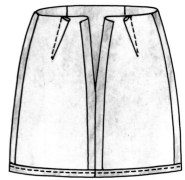

6 Make the lining by stitching the back
waist darts and center back seam. Stitch
the side seams and center front panel
seams. Leave an opening at the center
back for the zipper. Press all seams open.
Turn up ¼in (6mm) at the hem and a
further ⅜in (1cm) and baste. Stitch hem in
place close to inner edge. Press.

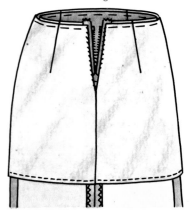

7 With the wrong sides together and
seams matching, insert the lining into
the skirt. Baste the skirt and lining
together around the waist edge. Slip-
stitch the lining to the skirt, turning in the
raw edges along the zipper.

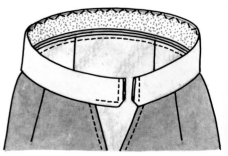

8 If interfacing waistband, catch-stitch
it along the foldline. Baste the interfacing
to the wrong side of the notched edge of
the waistband.

Cutting layout for skirt

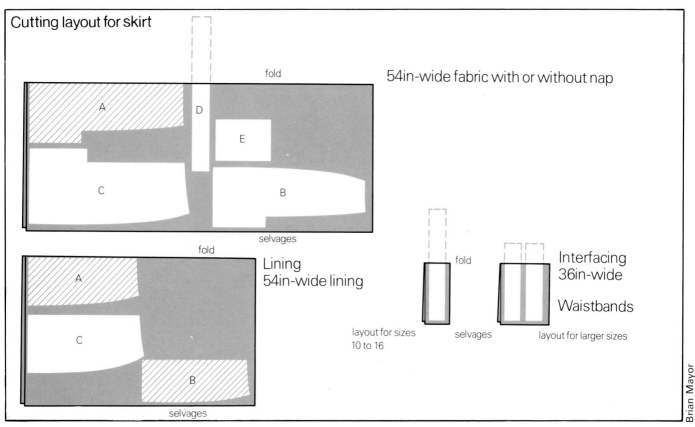

54in-wide fabric with or without nap

fold

A D

E

C B

selvages

Lining
54in-wide lining

fold

A

C

B

selvages

fold

selvages

layout for sizes
10 to 16

Interfacing
36in-wide

Waistbands

layout for larger sizes

Brian Mayor

9 Baste and stitch the interfaced edge of the waistband to the skirt. Grade the seam allowance, trimming the interfacing close to the stitching. Press seam toward the waist. Fold the waistband on the foldline with right sides together and stitch across the short ends. Clip corners and trim interfacing close to the stitching.

10 Turn the waistband to the right side. Turn under the raw edge on the inside of the waistband, enclosing all raw edges, and slip stitch to the stitching line at the waist edge. Press. Attach a skirt hook and eye to the waistband above the zipper.

Ross Greetham

79

Working with velvet

Velvet needs special handling because of its napped surface. Choose designs without too many style seams, such as a skirt or dress with unpressed pleats, as the velvet should be handled as little as possible during construction. Avoid patterns cut on the bias. Before cutting out the fabric it is important to adjust the pattern exactly; any alterations after cutting will affect the pile and are noticeable. If necessary, first make a muslin shell, to which adjustments can be made before the fabric is cut. Use silk thread for all pattern markings and basting stitches and fit the garment carefully before final stitching.

1 Lay the fabric on a flat surface with right side facing up. All the pattern pieces should be laid in one direction and with the pile running upward. Pile running downward will give a lighter look, which is more suitable for panne velvet. Use sharp dressmaker's pins, and pin between the seam allowance and the cutting edge to avoid marking the fabric.

2 Use a short ($\frac{1}{8}$in/3mm) stitch length and stitch with the pile: if the pile runs upward, stitch from the bottom to the top of the seam. Plain seams pressed open are the most suitable. To prevent velvet from slipping and wrinkling, stitch the seams with tissue paper between the two layers of velvet. Remove tissue after seam is stitched.

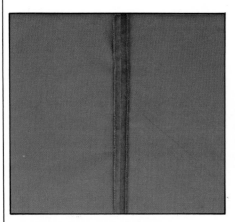

3 Finish seams with overcasting or zig-zag stitching. Insert zippers by hand using backstitch or hand picking. Wherever possible, use loops instead of buttonholes. Avoid stitching on the right side of the fabric; the presser foot will mark the surface.

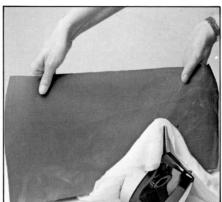

4 Before pressing, remove all basting stitches. To remove wrinkles, hold the garment over steam or hang it in a steam-filled bathroom. Never press velvet on the right side; this will flatten and mark the pile. A hot iron stood upright with a damp cloth over it will give enough steam to lift wrinkles from velvet when held close to the iron.

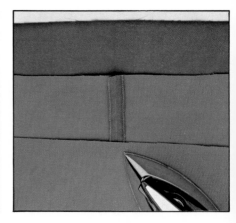

5 Press with the pile down on a needleboard; if this is not available, press with pile down on a piece of velvet with its pile facing up. For seams, use a press cloth made from a velvet scrap placed pile down on the seam. Pad the ironing board slightly with a clean cloth placed over a folded towel.

Flat ribbon button loops

Button loops made from ribbon are a simple and decorative way of fastening two edges together. They can be used on necklines, sleeves and front bodices of blouses, dresses and jackets. Made from delicate ribbon, they look very pretty on lingerie. They are best used with small buttons and most effective with shank buttons.

The ribbon loop consists of a miter made by folding the ribbon into a triangular shape.

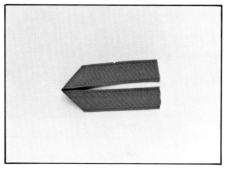

1 Lay a piece of ribbon flat and fold the top end across to the right so that an exact diagonal fold is made. Bring the lower end of the ribbon up and over to the right so that the sides of the ribbon meet at the center and a point is formed. Press the miter flat. This is the right side of the loop.

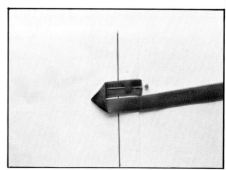

2 To determine the length of the ribbon required for each loop, make a paper diagram. Draw a line $\frac{5}{8}$in (1.5cm) from the edge to represent the seamline. Pin one end of the ribbon in place, matching the edge that represents the cutting line.

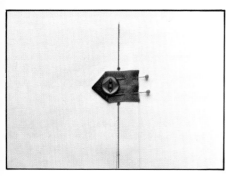

3 Make a loop around the button to be used and take the ribbon back to the cutting line. Make sure that the loop is big enough to extend beyond the seamline and over the button. Pin in place and trim excess ribbon; mark the seamline on each side of the loop; this will be the loop spacing.

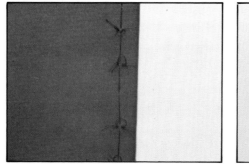

4 On the garment, mark the seamline with basting on the right-hand side. Lightly mark the spacing for the button loop as taken from the paper diagram. If the loops are continuous, mark the fabric at equal intervals. If they are separated, mark the position of each loop individually.

5 Cut the ribbon for each loop separately, taking the loop on the paper pattern as a master. Fold the ribbon to form loops and pin each loop in place. Slip stitch the loops together at the point so that they hold their shape until they are stitched.

6 Baste and stitch the loops with their right sides to the right side of the garment. Stitch $\frac{1}{8}$in (3mm) away from the seamline, within the seam allowance, making sure that the ends of the loops are on the cutting line. The stitching is not visible on the finished work. Remove pins and basting.

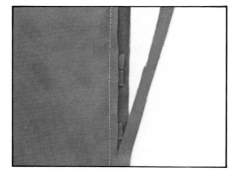

7 With right sides together and all edges matching, pin and baste the facing on the opening over the loops. Stitch the seam along the seamline $\frac{5}{8}$in (1.5cm) in from the edge. Trim the facing seam allowance and loop ends to $\frac{1}{4}$in (6mm), and the garment seam allowance to $\frac{3}{8}$in (1cm). Press seam allowance and stitching line only.

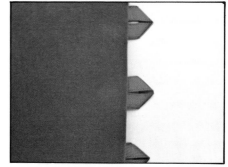

8 Turn the facing to the inside of the garment and press carefully on the folded edge. If basting first, use silk thread to prevent marking. Remove stitches from loops. When the facing is turned in, the loops will extend beyond the opening edge. For extra strength, a row of topstitching can be sewn close to the fold, but is not suitable for pile fabrics.

Decorative cord edging

This type of edging has a dual purpose: the loops can be used for fastening buttons and can also be continued on around an edge for decoration, as on the black dress on page 83. Many cords or braids are suitable, but the easiest for a beginner to use is a narrow flexible one. Start by marking the position for the loops on the garment as for flat ribbon loops. Measure the amount needed for each loop and mark the cord at these intervals.

1 Form the loops from one piece of cord by pinning in place and curving the cord around from the end of one loop ready to form the next loop. Baste and stitch loops within seam allowance.

2 Complete the edging with a facing as for flat ribbon loops. If you are using the loops with buttons, they should be sewn on the other edge to correspond with the loops.

Velvet dress

This dress is perfect for a night on the town. Make it in a luxurious fabric.

Adapting the pattern

The dress is made by adapting the basic dress pattern from the Stitch by Stitch Pattern Pack, available in sizes 10-20, which correspond to sizes 8-18 in ready-made clothes.

Materials
6 sheets of tracing paper 36 x 40in (90 x 100cm approx)
Yardstick, right triangle, flexible curve

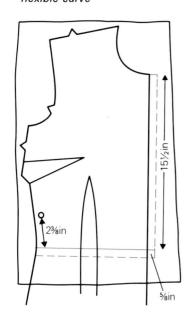

1 To make the front bodice pattern, mark the waistline on the basic dress pattern by

measuring down the center front edge from neck cutting line 15½in (39.5cm) for a size 10, adding an extra ¼in (6mm) to this measurement for each larger size. Draw a line across pattern at this point, at right angles to center front.

2 Lay tracing paper over the top half of the dress front pattern and trace the bodice to the waistline. Add a ⅝in (1.5cm) seam allowance to center front and waistline edge. The grain line is parallel to the center front. Mark the seamlines and bust dart. Mark the top zipper position 2⅜in (6cm) from the waist seamline on the side seamline.

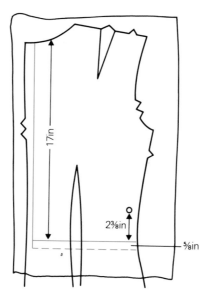

3 To make back bodice pattern, mark waistline on dress back pattern by measuring down center back seamline from back neck cutting line 17in (43.5cm) for a size 10, adding an extra ¼in (6mm) for each larger size.

4 Draw a line across the pattern at this point, at right angles to the center back. Trace the top half of the dress back to the waistline, omitting the center back seam allowance. The center back will be placed on a fold.

5 Add a ⅝in (1.5cm) seam allowance to waistline edge. The grain line is parallel to center back. Mark shoulder dart and top zipper position, 2⅜in (6cm) from waist seamline on side seamline.

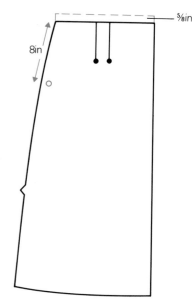

6 To make the skirt front, trace the bottom half of the basic dress pattern to the waistline edge. Add a ⅝in (.5cm) seam allowance to this edge. Mark the lower zipper position 8in (20cm) from waist seamline on side seamline. The center front (parallel to grain line) will be placed on a fold.

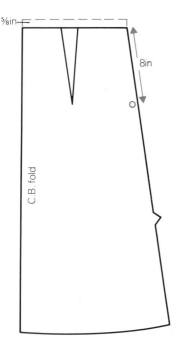

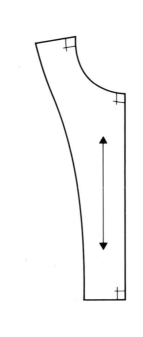

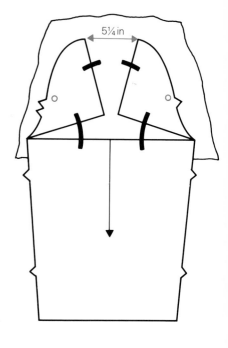

7 To make the skirt back pattern, trace the bottom half of the basic dress back to the waistline edge. Omit the center back seam allowance; this edge will be placed on a fold. Add ⅝in (1.5cm) seam allowance to the waist edge. Mark the bottom of the zipper 8in (20cm) below the waist seamline on the side seamline of the skirt.

9 Mark the ⅝in (1.5cm) seam allowances on the front, neck, shoulder and waist edges. The grain line is parallel to the center front edge. A ¼in (6mm) allowance has been included on the facing edge for finishing. This can be turned in and stitched, or left flat and overcast, according to the fabric used.

11 Lay the sleeve cap over the paper ready to tape in place. Slash from the center of the sleeve cap to the underarm line, and along this line to both side edges. Spread the sleeve cap, raising the upper section of the sleeve until the measurement between the two pieces at the sleeve cap is 5¼in (13cm). Tape in place.

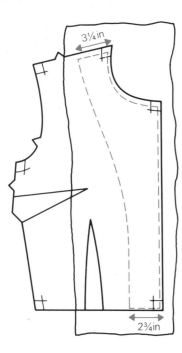

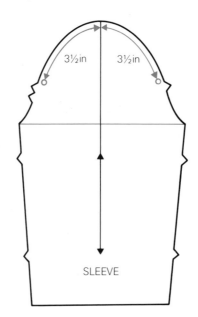

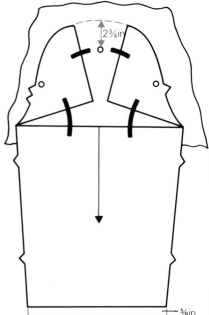

8 To make the front neck facing, lay tracing paper over the neck and front edge of the front bodice. Trace the neck and front edges along the shoulder 3¼in (8cm) and the waistline edge 2¾in (7cm). Using a flexible curve, connect these two points, keeping the line parallel to the front edge where possible.

10 To make the sleeve pattern, trace the basic dress sleeve, extending the grain line to the top of the sleeve cap. Omit the hem allowance. Mark the gathering points on the seamline around the sleeve cap 3½in (9cm) to each side of the center point. Draw a line across the pattern to connect the underarm seams at the armhole to provide a guide for spreading the sleeve.

12 Redraw the sleeve cap cutting line, making it 2¾in (7cm) above the original cutting line position. Add a ⅝in (1.5cm) seam allowance to the lower edge of the sleeve. Mark the grain line in the same position as on the lower half of the sleeve.

Chris Harvey

84

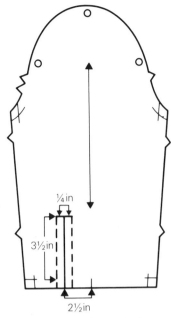

13 To mark the opening at the lower edge of the sleeve, measure from the center of the sleeve along the hem toward back of the sleeve, $2\frac{1}{2}$in (6.5cm) and mark. Draw a line parallel to the grain line $3\frac{1}{2}$in (9cm) long from the hem seamline. This is the center cutting line. On each side of this, draw another line $\frac{1}{4}$in (6mm) away from, and of equal length, to it. There are stitching lines of the opening.

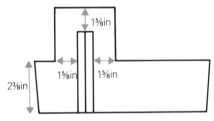

14 To make the hem and opening facing, lay tracing paper over the lower edge of the sleeve and trace the stitching and cutting lines of the opening. Trace the lower edge of the sleeve and up the underarm on each side for $2\frac{3}{8}$in (6cm). Draw a line parallel to the hem edge from these points, taking it to within $1\frac{5}{8}$in (4cm) of each side of the opening and up beyond the top of the opening by $1\frac{5}{8}$in (4cm).

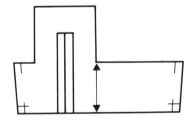

15 Mark the seam allowances and the grain line parallel to the opening, and cut out this piece for the facing. Mark the front of the sleeve on the facing piece. This pattern piece will be cut out twice.

Chris Harvey

16 To make the belt pattern, draw a rectangle $36\frac{1}{2} \times 8$in (93 x 20cm) for sizes 10, 12; $39\frac{1}{2} \times 8$in (100 x 20cm) for sizes 14, 16; and 42 x 8in (107 x 20cm) for sizes 18, 20. Fold rectangle in two along length, marking foldline. Measure in along top line $4\frac{3}{4}$in (12cm) and mark. Repeat with lower line; join the marks to form a point. The other end is placed on fold.

17 For the interfacing position, draw a vertical line 7in (18cm) in from center front edge, from center foldline to one edge. Add a $\frac{5}{8}$in (1.5cm) seam allowance around all edges except the center front.

Directions for making

Materials

36in (90cm)-wide fabric with nap:
Sizes 10, 12: 3⅝yd (3.3m)
Sizes 14, 16: 3¾yd (3.4cm)
Sizes 18, 20: 3⅞yd (3.5m)
36in (90cm)-wide moiré for belt
Sizes 10. 12: 2¼yd (2m)
Sizes 14, 16: 2⅜yd (2.1m)
Sizes 18, 20: 2½yd (2.2m)
36in (90cm)-wide interfacing:
for all sizes: ⅝yd (.6m)
Matching thread
10in (25cm) dress zipper
Buttons to fasten front and sleeves
Decorative cord or ribbon for front and
sleeve fastenings (edging optional)

Key to adapted pattern pieces

A Front bodice   Cut 2
B Back bodice   Cut 1 on fold
C Skirt front   Cut 1 on fold
D Skirt back   Cut 1 on fold
E Front neck facing   Cut 2
F Back neck facing   Cut 1 on fold
G Sleeve   Cut 2
H Sleeve facing   Cut 2
I Belt   Cut 1 on fold
Interfacing: use pieces E Cut 2, F Cut 1
on fold, I Cut to pattern measurement.

Suggested fabrics

Velvet, velveteen, velour, satin, brocade,
heavy taffeta.

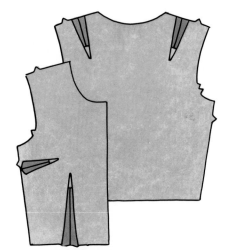

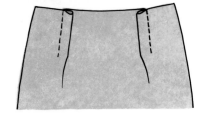

1 With right sides together, fold, baste and
stitch front and side bust darts, front and
back waist dart and shoulder darts. Cut
through the center of the darts and finish
the raw edges by overcasting. Press
darts open. Fold, baste and stitch the skirt
front darts and press toward the center.
For pressing velvet, see page 80.

2 Measure the size of the loops needed
and mark the loop positions along the
center front edge of the right front bodice
as shown on page 81. Pin, baste and
stitch the loops in place on the right
side.

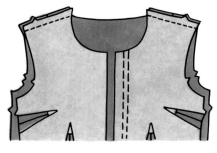

3 Stitch the shoulder seams, right sides
together. Finish and press open.

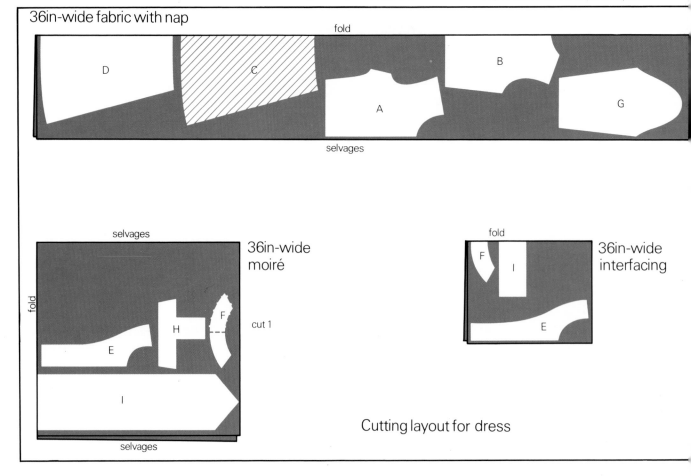

36in-wide fabric with nap

fold

D   C   A   B   G

selvages

selvages

fold

36in-wide moiré

H   E   F

cut 1

I

selvages

fold

F   I

36in-wide interfacing

E

Cutting layout for dress

4 Baste the interfacing to the wrong side of the front and back neck facings. With right sides together, baste and stitch the neck facings together at the shoulder seams. Trim the interfacing close to the stitching. Press seams open. Finish the outer edge of the facing by overcasting or turning in $\frac{1}{4}$in (6mm) and stitching, if the fabric is thin enough.

5 With right sides together, pin and baste the facings to the neck edge and front edges of the bodice over the loops. Stitch entire seam, taking $\frac{5}{8}$in (1.5cm) seam allowances. Grade allowances, trimming interfacing close to stitching. Clip neck curves and front corners.

6 Turn the facings to the inside of the garment. Baste close to the folded edge and press carefully. Remove basting. Catch-stitch facings to the shoulder seams and baste the facing to the waist edge within the seam allowance.

7 With right sides together and center fronts matching, baste and stitch the skirt front to the bodice fronts. Matching

center fronts and center backs, baste and stitch the skirt back to the bodice back. Trim the interfacing at the front. Trim the seam allowances, overcast them together and press upward.

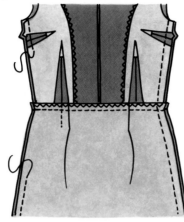

8 With right sides together, baste and stitch the left side seam only, leaving the opening for zipper. Press the seam open and finish the edges with overcasting. Insert zipper into opening by hand. With right sides together, baste and stitch the right side seam. Press seam open and finish edges.

9 Mark the stitching lines at the sleeve opening with basting stitches. Make loops to the same measurement as on the front opening and pin and baste the loops to the front side of the sleeve opening in the positions marked, so that the ends of the loops are on the cutting line of the opening with the points facing toward the front of the sleeve.

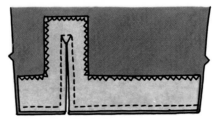

10 Finish the inner edges of the sleeve facing by overcasting. With right sides together, pin and baste the facing to the

sleeve, covering loops and matching center line of the opening. With wrong side of sleeve up, stitch the facing to the sleeve around the opening following the basting lines.

11 Cut along the center of the opening to within $\frac{3}{8}$in (1cm) of the inner end. Cut diagonally into the corners. Do not cut through the stitching. Trim seam around sleeve hem and cut across corners.

12 Turn the facing to the inside of the sleeve, baste close to the fold and press. Remove basting stitches, pull the facing down flat and, with right sides together, stitch the underarm seam and facing in one piece.
Finish the seams.

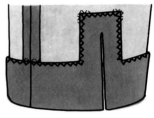

Terry Evans

13 Turn the facing to the inside. Press again and catch-stitch the interfacing to the sleeve on the seam and on the corners of the opening. Run two rows of gathering stitches between marks on sleeve cap. Pull up gathers to fit the armhole.

14 With right sides together and seams, notches and shoulder points matching, pin the sleeve into the armhole. Baste the sleeve in place, spreading the gathers evenly over the sleeve cap. Stitch the sleeve in place. Trim seam and clip underarm curves, overcast the seam together and press toward sleeve. Repeat the last steps with other sleeve.

15 Turn up the hem and complete, following the directions given for the basic dress. Alternatively, use the straight binding method (see Volume 3, page 63), which is more suitable for a thick pile fabric such as velvet. Sew buttons on front and sleeves of dress to match loops.

16 Baste the interfacing to the wrong side of the belt within the front area marked on the pattern. Catch-stitch the interfacing to the foldline. With right sides together, fold belt in half along foldline and baste. Stitch $\frac{5}{8}$in (1.5cm) in from open edge leaving 6in (15cm) open near center to turn. Trim seams and clip corners.

17 Turn belt right side out through the opening. Slip-stitch the opening edges together. Baste close to the edges and press carefully. Remove basting stitches. The stiffened area of the belt is worn at the front of the waist; the belt ends are taken to the back, crossed over and brought around to the front where they are tied in a knot.
Or, wrap the belt around the waist once and tie it in a loose bow or sash at back or front.

*Trapunto quilting
*Working trapunto quilting
*Trapunto designs
*A trapunto-quilted vest

Trapunto quilting

In Needlework course 3 we showed you how to do the most familiar kind of quilting, in which a layer of padding is sandwiched between two layers of fabric and the three layers stitched together in a decorative pattern. In this course we introduce a purely decorative kind of quilting called "trapunto" (from the Italian word *trapuntare*, "to quilt"). In trapunto only the motif is padded—though, of course, a trapunto-quilted garment can be interlined with batting to make it warm.

The technique is simple: a design is stitched through the main fabric and a backing fabric, then slits are cut in the backing, in the areas to be padded, and stuffing is inserted, producing a relief effect on the right side.

As in ordinary quilting, the top fabric should be closely woven but soft. We used silk honan for the vest shown on page 90; other suitable fabrics include broadcloth, poplin, shantung and satin. Solid colors are usually preferable, as they permit the design to be clearly seen, but you can create an interesting effect by quilting the motifs on a printed fabric.

The backing fabric should be thin: batiste, voile, organdy and cheesecloth are good choices.

A lining is needed to hide the underside of the work. Your choice of lining depends mainly on what you are making. For the vest we used a lightweight silk lining fabric in a matching color. If you were making a pillow cover, a plain fabric in a neutral color would do.

For the padding polyester stuffing is ideal. You can also use bits of thick polyester batting, teased out from the main piece.

If you are stitching the design by machine, use ordinary sewing thread matching the fabric in type and color (or perhaps a little darker). For hand quilting use either ordinary sewing thread or quilting thread, which is glossier and less apt to knot.

An embroidery frame is useful if you are quilting by hand, as it permits you to make very small running stitches, using a stabbing motion, to produce a fine line.

Working trapunto quilting

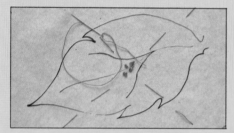

1 First baste the main fabric and the backing together, working across the fabrics vertically and horizontally, then around the edges. Then baste the tracing of the design to the right side of the main fabric as shown, working outward from the center in a star pattern. Knot the end of the thread and finish each line with a single backstitch.

2 Using a small straight stitch, machine stitch the design lines through tracing paper and fabric. In turning corners, lower the needle first, then raise the presser foot and pivot the work. In intricate parts of the design you may need to turn the hand wheel manually.

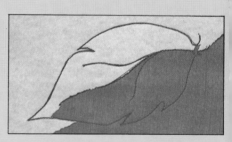

3 Pull the upper threads through to the underside and tie them and the bobbin threads together securely. Or sew the threads into the backing fabric. Remove all basting threads except those around the edges. Gently pull away the tracing. You may find this easier if you first run a fine needle along the stitching. Use tweezers to remove stubborn bits of paper.

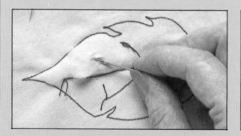

4 Make a small slit in the backing and insert a small amount of stuffing into the opening. Use the blunt end of a large tapestry needle to push the stuffing into the corners. Use enough to round the shape; avoid over-stuffing.

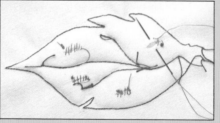

5 Using ordinary sewing thread, sew the edges of the slit together. Do not pull the stitches too hard.

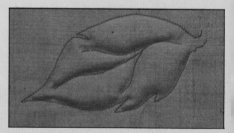

6 The quilted motif stands up in relief against the surrounding fabric. When the quilting is completed, the garment or other object is assembled and lined.

The important thing to remember in designing trapunto is to keep the individual shapes fairly small and simple, so that you can achieve a smoothly-padded effect. Notice how the designer of the vest shown here has divided the large leaves into sections with veins and stuffed these sections individually.

To add contrast to your design, include some lines of stitching and unpadded shapes—such as the upper parts of the buds on the vest. If you like, you can highlight parts of the design with embroidery stitches and/or beads.

John Hutchinson

89

Festive wear

Trapunto-quilted blossoms and leaves, embellished with French knots and beads, give a rich texture to this red silk vest.

Size The vest shown is size 10 (size 8 in ready-made clothes) but the pattern can be adapted for sizes 12, 14 and 16. A seam allowance of $\frac{5}{8}$in (1.5cm) is included.

Materials

- $1\frac{1}{8}$yd (1m) of 45in (115cm)-wide fabric, or $1\frac{1}{2}$yd (1.5m) of 36in (90cm)-wide fabric—for all sizes
- $\frac{5}{8}$yd (.6m) of 45in (115cm)-wide lining fabric (all sizes)
- Backing fabric, such as cheesecloth or voile (same amount as of lining)
- Sewing thread in a shade slightly darker than fabric (use silk thread on silk fabric), or quilting thread for hand quilting
- Matching sewing thread
- Small amount of polyester stuffing or batting
- Small amount of embroidery thread, such as stranded floss or pearl cotton
- A few beads (optional)
- Embroidery hoop (optional)
- $4\frac{1}{4}$yd (3.8m) of $\frac{1}{8}$in (3mm)-diameter filler cord (a little more for larger sizes)
- 12 small buttons
- Graph paper ruled in 1in (2.5cm) squares
- Tracing paper
- Medium-sized crewel needle
- Large tapestry needle
- Beading needle (optional)
- Sharp embroidery scissors
- Dressmaker's carbon paper (for hand quilting)

Preparing the fabric

1 Using the graph paper and the method described in Needlework course 6, Volume 4, page 76, enlarge the vest pattern shown opposite. Make the necessary adaptations (given with pattern) for sizes 12, 14 or 16. Cut out the pattern pieces.
2 Cut out the vest in all three fabrics (having first pressed the fabrics), placing the pieces lengthwise and on the straight grain of the fabric. Put the lining pieces aside.
3 Place each vest front piece, right side up, on the corresponding backing fabric piece. Baste them together carefully down the center of the piece, then baste again horizontally across the center. Add a few more lines of vertical and horizontal basting and, finally, baste around edges.
4 Baste the back section to the

corresponding backing piece with only one vertical and one horizontal line, plus the line around the edge.
5 Using tailor's tacks, mark the positions of the darts.

Quilting

1 Trace the quilting motif twice.
2 Pin each tracing to a front piece (reversing the design on the left front), positioning the lowest petal about 1in (2.5cm) above the lower point of the

seamline and the large bud the same distance from the front seamline.
3 Baste the tracings in place, working outward from the center as shown in step 1, page 88. (Or, if you are hand-quilting the design, transfer it to the backing fabric—reversing it first—using dressmaker's carbon.)
4 Before stitching the design, work a small sample, using a piece of backing fabric, main fabric and tracing paper. Using a small stitch, work back and

forth. Tear away the tracing paper and adjust the stitch length and tension if necessary.

5 Now stitch the design as shown in step 2, page 88, stitching slowly and carefully. Try to organize stitching to give a minimum of starts and stops.

Quilting by hand Place the front piece in the embroidery frame, backing fabric upward. Quilt along the lines using a small, neat running stitch. Take care to begin and finish off the threads securely.

6 Remove the basting threads and insert the stuffing as shown in steps 3 and 4, page 88. Sew up the slits in the backing fabric as shown in step 5.

7 For the flower centers, work French knots (see Volume 5, page 76), using embroidery thread and, preferably, an embroidery hoop. For an extra-rich effect sew a few beads among the knots.

Assembling the vest

1 Pin and baste the darts in the front sections and adjust them, if necessary, to fit your figure. Remember that the vest must fit over a blouse or sweater. Stitch the darts and press them down.

2 Pin and baste the shoulder seams, adjust the fit if necessary and stitch the

seams. Press seams open.

3 Repeat steps 1 and 2 on the lining pieces.

4 From the main fabric cut enough bias strips, each 1½in (4cm) wide, to make a strip 4¾yd (4.3m) long. Stitch the pieces together on the straight grain, and press seams open. Cut off 48in (122cm) of the bias strip to be used for button loops.

5 Fold the remaining piece of bias around the filler cord, right side out and raw edges even. Using the zipper foot of the machine, stitch close to the cord along the entire length. Cut off the excess cord.

6 Cut a piece of cording to fit the lower back edge of the vest. Lay it along the seamline with the cord upward, just outside the seam allowance. Baste and stitch it in place using the zipper foot. Repeat along the other edges of the vest—except the side seams—clipping the seam allowance of the cording at corners and along curves to achieve a smooth fit and so that the seam allowances will lie flat.

7 For the button loops make corded tubing as follows: cut a 56in (142cm) piece of cord. Fold the 28in (71cm) bias strip around half the length of the cord, wrong side out. With zipper foot on the machine, stitch first across the inner end

of the bias strip to anchor it to the middle of the cord, and then along the length of the cord, close to it, stretching the fabric slightly. Trim the seam. Turn tubing right side out by turning back right side of fabric and at the same time pulling on the covered end of the cord until the other half of the cord is covered. Trim away the excess cord including the stitched end.

8 Cut 12 short pieces of corded tubing to fit your buttons, allowing enough to go around the button in a "U" shape, plus about 1in (2.5cm) extra.

9 Baste the loops firmly in place over the

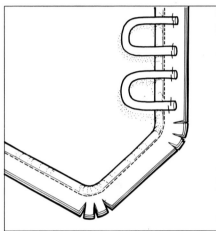

cording on the right front edge, as shown, beginning 1¾in (4.5cm) above the lower seamline and ending just below the neckline, spacing them evenly. After basting the first loop, check it over a button to make sure it fits. Use backstitch for basting to make sure the loops stay in place while the lining is being attached.

10 Lay the lining over the vest, right sides together and raw edges matching. Pin the two layers together along all the corded edges. Baste and stitch, using zipper foot. Grade the seam allowances and clip curves.

11 Turn the vest right side out by pulling the front pieces through the shoulders and out of one side opening in back.

12 Press the vest carefully around the edges, using a pressing cloth and avoiding the quilted areas.

13 Pin the side edges of the vest together, omitting the lining. Baste and stitch, starting and finishing just where the cording joins the garment. Press the seam open and tuck the ends of the cording under the lining as neatly as possible.

14 Smooth the front lining seam allowances over the side seams so that they lie flat. Fold under each back lining seam allowance so that the fold lies over the side seam and overlaps the front lining seam allowance. Baste along the fold, press and sew the back lining to the front, using hemming stitch.

15 On the left front, sew buttons to correspond with the button loops.

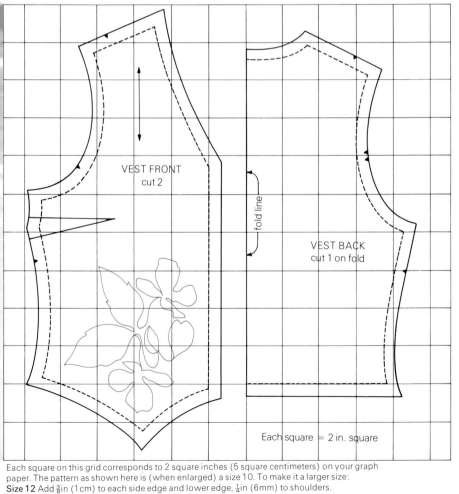

VEST FRONT
cut 2

fold line

VEST BACK
cut 1 on fold

Each square = 2 in. square

Each square on this grid corresponds to 2 square inches (5 square centimeters) on your graph paper. The pattern as shown here is (when enlarged) a size 10. To make it a larger size:
Size 12 Add ⅜in (1cm) to each side edge and lower edge, ¼in (6mm) to shoulders.
Size 14 Add ⅞in (2.2cm) to each side edge and lower edge, ½in (1.2cm) to shoulders.
Size 16 Add 1⅜in (3.5cm) to each side edge and lower edge, ¾in (2cm) to shoulders.

EXTRA SPECIAL CROCHET

This overall-style pinafore will appeal to any fashion-conscious girl. It's quick to crochet and can be worn day in and day out.

Best bib and tucker

Peter Waldman

Sizes
To fit 24[26:28]in (61[66:71]cm) chest.
Skirt length, 10[12½:15]in (25[32:38]cm).
Note: Directions for larger sizes are in brackets []; if there is only one set of figures it applies to all sizes.

Materials
8[9:10]oz (200[225:250]g) of a knitting worsted
Sizes E and F (3.50 and 4.00mm) crochet hooks
2 overall fasteners

Gauge
18 hdc to 4in (10cm) worked on size F (4.00mm) hook.

Back
Using size F (4.00mm) hook make 73[77:81]ch.
Base row 1 hdc into 3rd ch from hook, 1 hdc into each ch to end. Turn.
Patt row 2ch to count as first hdc, 1 hdc into each hdc to end, 1 hdc into top of 2ch. Turn. 72[76:80] hdc.

Rep last row 1 [2:3] times more.
Dec row 2ch, 1 hdc into each of next 17[18:19] hdc, dec 1 hdc by working 2hdc tog, 1 hdc into each hdc to within last 20[21:22] hdc, dec 1 hdc, 1 hdc into each hdc to end. Turn.
Work 3[4:5] rows straight. Rep last 4[5:6] rows until 58[62:66] hdc rem; end with a dec row. Cont straight until skirt measures 10[12½:15]in (25[32:38]cm). Fasten off.

Front
Work as for back.
Bib
Skip first 19[20:21] sts at top of front, rejoin yarn to next st and using size F (4.00mm) hook, work 2ch, 1 hdc into each of next 19[21:23] hdc, turn. Work in patt for 3½[4¼:5½]in (9[11:14]cm). Fasten off.
Pockets (make 2)
Using size F (4.00mm) hook make 19ch. Work base row as for back, then work 12 rows in patt. Fasten off.
Edging
Using size E (3.50mm) hook join yarn to

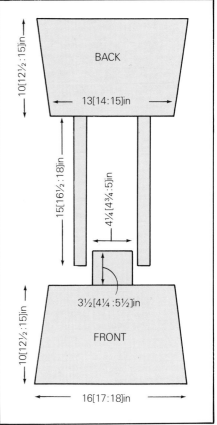

John Hutchinson

first of foundation ch and work 1 sc into each ch, 3sc into corner, now work 1 sc into each row end to next corner, 3sc into corner, 1 sc into each st to next corner, 3sc into corner, 1 sc into each row end to corner, 3sc into corner, sl st into first sc. Fasten off.
Straps (make 2)
Using size E (3.50mm) hook make 7ch.
Base row 1 sc into 2nd ch from hook, 1 sc into each ch to end. Turn.
Next row 1 ch, 1 sc into each sc to end. Turn. Rep last row until strap measures 15[16½:18]in (38[42:46]cm). Fasten off.

To finish
Join side seams of skirt.
Bib edging
Using size E (3.50mm) hook and with RS facing join yarn to first row end of left side of bib, work 1 sc into each row end up side of bib to corner, 3sc into corner, 1 sc into each st to next corner, 3sc into corner then 1 sc into each row end along other side of bib, turn. Work 2 rows sc around bib, working 3sc at corners. Fasten off.
Waist edging
Using size E (3.50mm) hook join on yarn and work 1 row sc evenly around top edge of skirt. Fasten off.
Lower edging
Using size E (3.50mm) hook join on yarn and work 1 row sc evenly around lower edge of skirt. Fasten off.
Attach one end of straps to skirt back; place fastener at other end. Attach stud to bib corners. Sew pockets to skirt front.

Indoors . . . outdoors

This jacket, crocheted in a thick yarn with a knitted waistband ribbing, is the perfect choice for casual wear.

Sizes
To fit 36[38:40:42:44]in (92[97:102:107:112]cm) chest.
Length, 30½[31:31½:32:32½]in (77.5[79:80:81:82.5]cm).
Sleeve seam, 18¼[18¼:18¾:19¼:19¼]in (46[46:47:48.5:48.5]cm).
Note Directions for larger sizes are in brackets [ ]; if there is only one set of figures it applies to all sizes.

Materials
43[46:50:50:53]oz (1200[1300:1400:1400:1500]g) of a bulky-weight yarn
Size 15 (9.00mm) crochet hook
No. 10½ (7mm) knitting needles
9 buttons

Gauge
7dc to 4in (10cm) and 5 rows to 4½in (11.5cm) worked on size 15 (9.00mm) hook.

Back
Using hook make 37[39:41:43:45]ch.
Base row 1dc into 3rd ch from hook, 1dc into each ch to end. Turn.
Patt row 2ch to count as first dc, 1dc into each st to end. Turn. 36[38:40:42:44] dc.
Rep patt row until work measures 27½[28:28½:29:29½]in (70[71.5:72.5:73.5:75]cm). Fasten off.

Left front
Using hook make 16[17:18:19:20] ch and work base row and patt row as for back. 15[16:17:18:19] dc. Cont in patt until front is 1 row less than back.
Shape neck
Fasten off. Skip first 6[6:7:7:7]dc, rejoin yarn to next st, 2ch, work to end. Fasten off.

Right front
Work as left front to neck shaping.
Shape neck
Work to last 6[6:7:7:7]dc. Fasten off.

Sleeves
Using hook make 25[27:29:31:33]ch and work base row and patt row as for back. Cont in patt, inc one st at each end of next and every foll 3rd row until there are 34[36:38:40:42] sts. Cont straight until sleeve measures 15[15:15½:16:16]in (38[38:39:40.5:40.5]cm). Fasten off.

Cuffs
Using needles pick up and K one st from each foundation ch along lower edge of sleeve. 24[26:28:30:32] sts. Work in K2, P2 ribbing for 3¼in (8cm). Bind off in ribbing.

Back waistband
Using needles pick up and K sts along foundation ch of lower edge thus: *K1, inc in next ch, K1 into next ch, K1 between ch, rep from * to end. Now work 3in (7.5cm) in K2, P2 ribbing.

Front waistbands
Work as for back waistband.

Button band
With RS facing using needles pick up and K 60[64:68:72:76] sts along front edge and work 6 rows in K2, P2 ribbing. Bind off in ribbing.

Buttonhole band
With RS facing using needles pick up and K 60[64:68:72:76] sts along front edge and work 2 rows in K2, P2 ribbing.
1st buttonhole row Rib 3[5:4:6:5], *bind off 1, rib until there are 8[8:9:9:10] sts on right-hand needle after bound-off st, rep from * 5 times, rib to end.
2nd buttonhole row Work in K2, P2 ribbing casting on one st over bound-off st of previous row.
Now work 2 more rows in K2, P2 ribbing. Bind off in ribbing.

Collar
Join shoulder seams. With RS of work facing skip top of button band and pick up and K 14[15:16:17:18] sts along right front neck, along back as for waistband, and 14[15:16:17:18] sts along left front neck omitting top of buttonhole band. Work 24 rows in K2, P2 ribbing.
Next row Rib 3, bind off 1, rib to last 4 sts, bind off 1, rib 2.
Next row Rib casting on one st over bound-off sts.
Work 1 more row in K2, P2 ribbing, then bind off loosely in ribbing.

To finish
Mark top edge of sleeves at center; with center of sleeves to shoulder seam, sew sleeves to fronts and back, then join side and sleeve seams. Sew on buttons.

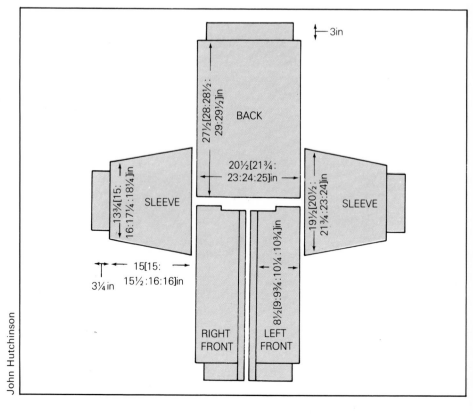

John Hutchinson

Technique tip

Splicing

When working in rows, always join in a new ball of yarn at the beginning of a row. If the yarn has to be joined in the middle of the work, which is necessary when working in rounds, or if the yarn is very thick, the old ball of yarn and the new ball should be spliced together.

If you do this neatly, the joined ends of yarn will be invisible and therefore you will not need to darn in loose ends after you have completed the garment. In the pictures below, the ends of old and new yarn are shown in contrasting colors for clarity.

To do this, divide the end of each ball of yarn in half and unravel for approximately $2\frac{1}{4}$in (6cm). The yarn shown here has only two strands; some yarns have more.

Cut away, at an angle, half of the strands from each end. Trim the remaining long ends in the same way. Then overlay the two ends from opposite directions so that the long strands overlap.

Twist the strands together until they hold. The twisted section should be of the same thickness as the original yarn. The trimmed ends should butt together to give a neat finish.

Coral Mula

A night on the town

Sequins sewn on the shoulders add extra sparkle to this lacy evening cardigan, which is perfect for festive occasions. It can be worn either loose or bloused and looks great with skirt or pants.

Sizes
To fit 36-38in (92-97cm) bust.
Length, 25in (64cm).
Sleeve seam, 17in (43cm).

Materials
11oz (300g) of a sport yarn
1 pair each Nos. 2 and 3 (3 and 3¼mm) knitting needles
4 buttons
Leaf sequins

Gauge
28 sts and 36 rows to 4in (10cm) in stockinette st on No. 3 (3¼mm) needles.

Back
Using No. 2 (3mm) needles cast on 102 sts.
1st row *K1 tbl, P1, rep from * to end.
Rep this row until work measures 4in (10cm). Change to No. 3 (3¼mm) needles. P 1 row and K 1 row, inc one st at center of last row. 103 sts. Beg patt.
1st and every alternate row (WS) P.
2nd row K3, *yo, sl 1 knitwise, K1, psso, K4, rep from * to last 4 sts, yo, sl 1 knitwise, K1, psso, K2.
4th row K1, *K2 tog, yo, K1, yo, sl 1 knitwise, K1, psso, K1, rep from * to end.
6th row K2 tog, yo, *K3, yo, sl 1 knitwise, K2 tog, psso, yo, rep from * to last 5 sts, K3, yo, sl 1 knitwise, K1, psso.
8th row K1, *yo, sl 1 knitwise, K1, psso, K1, K2 tog, yo, K1, rep from * to end.
10th row As 8th.
These 10 rows form patt. Rep them 3 times more.
Cont in patt, inc one st at each end of next and every foll 4th row until there are 115 sts, working increased sts in stockinette st. Cont straight until work measures 25in (64cm); end with a P row. Bind off. Place a marker in 43rd st from each end.

Left front
Using No. 2 (3mm) needles cast on 44 sts. Work 4in (10cm) ribbing as for back. Change to No. 3 (3¼mm) needles. P 1 row and K 1 row, inc one st in center of last row. 45 sts. Beg patt.
1st and every alternate row (WS) P.
2nd row K3, *yo, sl 1 knitwise, K1, psso, K4, rep from * to last 6 sts, yo, sl 1 knitwise, K1, psso, K4.
4th row K1, *K2 tog, yo, K1, yo, sl 1 knitwise, K1, psso, K1, rep from * to last 2 sts, K2.
6th row K2 tog, yo, *K3, yo, sl 1 knitwise, K2 tog, psso, yo, rep from * to last 7 sts, K3, yo, sl 1 knitwise, K1, psso, K2.
8th row K1, *yo, sl 1 knitwise, K1, psso, K1, K2 tog, yo, K1, rep from * to last 2 sts, K2.
10th row As 8th.
These 10 rows form patt. Cont in patt, inc one st at side edge of next and every foll 4th row until there are 51 sts, working increased sts in patt. Cont straight until work measures 25in (64cm); end with a RS row.
Next row P4, (P2 tog, P4) 7 times, P2 tog, P3. 43 sts. Bind off.

Right front
Using No. 2 (3mm) needles cast on 44 sts. Work 4in (10cm) ribbing as for back. Change to No. 3 (3¼mm) needles. P 1 row and K1 row, inc one st in center of last row. 45 sts. Beg patt.
1st and every alternate row (WS) P.
2nd row K5, *yo, sl 1 knitwise, K1, psso, K4, rep from * to last 4 sts, yo, sl 1 knitwise, K1, psso, K2.
4th row K3, *K2 tog, yo, K1, yo, sl 1 knitwise, K1, psso, K1, rep from * to end.
6th row K2, K2 tog, yo, *K3, yo, sl 1 knitwise, K2 tog, psso, yo, rep from * to last 5 sts, K3, yo, sl 1 knitwise, K1, psso.
8th row K3, *yo, sl 1 knitwise, K1, psso, K1, K2 tog, yo, K1, rep from * to end.
10th row As 8th.
These 10 rows form patt. Cont in patt, inc one st at side edge of next and every foll 4th row until there are 51 sts, working increased sts in patt. Cont straight until work measures 25in (64cm); end with a

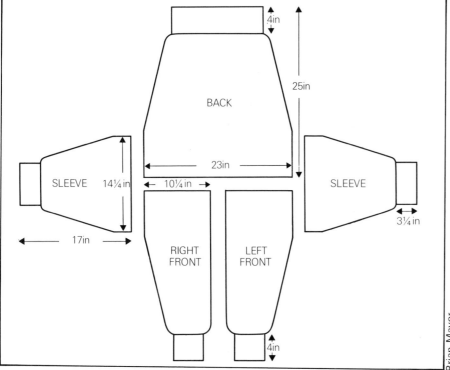

BACK

4in

25in

23in

10¼in

SLEEVE   14¼in

17in

SLEEVE

3¼in

RIGHT FRONT

LEFT FRONT

4in

Brian Mayor

RS row.

Next row P3, (P2 tog, P4) 7 times, P2 tog, P4. 43 sts.
Bind off.

Sleeves

Using No. 2 (3mm) needles cast on 60 sts. Work $3\frac{1}{4}$in (8cm) ribbing as for back. Change to No. 3 ($3\frac{1}{4}$mm) needles. P 1 row and K1 row, inc one st at center of last row. 61 sts. Cont in patt as for back, inc one st at each end of the 6th and every foll 5th row until there are 91 sts. Cont without shaping until work measures 17in (43cm) ending with a P row. Bind off.

Front band

Join shoulder seams. Using No. 2 (3mm) needles cast on 10 sts.
Work 3 rows ribbing as for back.
Next row (buttonhole row) Rib 4, bind off 2 sts, rib to end.
Next row Rib to end, casting on 2 sts over those bound off in previous row. Cont in ribbing, making 3 more buttonholes at intervals of $3\frac{1}{4}$in (8cm), until band, when slightly stretched, fits up right front, around the back of the neck and down the left front.
Bind off in ribbing.

To finish

Block the work.
Placing center of bound-off edge of sleeve to shoulder seam, sew sleeve top in position. Join side and sleeve seams.
Sew on sequins into center of alternate patterns as shown in photograph below.
Sew on buttons.

We've used pure wool in natural shades echoing the colors of the autumn countryside to knit a beautiful hooded coat which any child would be delighted to wear.

Woodland fantasy

Rod Delroy

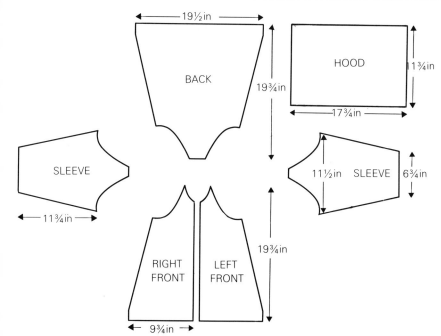

Diagram measurements:
- BACK: 19½in (top), 19¾in (side)
- HOOD: 17¾in (bottom), 1¾in (side)
- SLEEVE (left): 11¾in
- SLEEVE (right): 11½in, 6¾in
- RIGHT FRONT / LEFT FRONT: 9¾in, 19¾in

Sizes

To fit 25-28in (64-70cm) chest.
Length, 19¾in (50cm).
Sleeve seam, 11¾in (30cm).

Materials

24oz (650g) of a sport yarn in main color (A)
4oz (100g) in contrasting color (B)
2oz (50g) in each of contrasting colors (C, D and E)
1 pair each Nos. 3 and 6 (3¼ and 4½mm) knitting needles
6 toggles

Gauge

20 sts and 28 rows to 4in (10cm) in stockinette st on No. 6 (4½mm) needles.

Back

Using No. 3 (3¼mm) needles and A, cast on 97 sts. Beg with a P row, work 1½in (4cm) reverse stockinette st; end with a K row. Change to No. 6 (4½mm) needles.
Next row K1, *P23, K1, rep from * to end.
Next row P1, *K23, P1, rep from * to end.
Rep last 2 rows for 1½in (4cm); end with a K row. Beg shaping for patt.
1st row K1, P23, K1, P19, turn.
**2nd row K19, P1, K19, turn.
3rd row P18, P into front and back of next st—called Pfb—, K1, Pfb, P14, turn.
4th row K16, P1, K16, turn.
5th row P15, Pfb, K1, Pfb, P11, turn.
6th row K13, P1, K13, turn.
7th row P12, Pfb, K1, Pfb, P8, turn.
8th row K10, P1, K10, turn.
9th row P9, Pfb, K1, Pfb, P5, turn.
10th row K7, P1, K7, turn.
11th row P6, Pfb, K1, Pfb, P2, turn.
12th row K4, P1, K4, turn.**
13th row P3, Pfb, K1, Pfb, P27. K1, P23, K1, P19, turn.

Rep from ** to **.
25th row P3, Pfb, K1, Pfb, P27, K1. 121 sts.
26th row P to end.
27th row Using B and C, working in patt from chart overleaf, K1, *sl 1, K1, psso, K27, pick up loop lying between needles and K tbl—called make 1 (M1)—, K1, M1, K27, K2 tog, K1, rep from * once more.
28th row Working in patt from chart, P to end.
Rep last 2 rows 5 times more, then 27th row again. Break off B and C. Cont in A.
40th row P to end.
41st row K1, *P2 tog tbl, P27, K1, P27, P2 tog, K1, rep from * once more. 117 sts.
42nd row P1, *K28, P1, rep from * 3 times more.
43rd row K1, *P2 tog tbl, P25, Pfb, K1, Pfb, P25, P2 tog, K1, rep from * once more.
Rep last 2 rows 4 times more, then 42nd row again.
53rd row K1, *P2 tog tbl, P26, K1, P26, P2 tog, K1, rep from * once more. 113 sts.
54th row P to end.
55th row Using D and E and working in patt from chart, K1, *sl 1, K1, psso, K25, M1, K1, M1, K25, K2 tog, K1, rep from * once more.
Note: On this and foll patt panels, start rows in same place as on last panel. Allow for smaller no. of sts by working as far as "M1, K1, M1", then skip appropriate no. of sts here to ensure that patt matches at each side of center "K1."
56th row Working in patt from chart, P to end.
Rep last 2 rows 5 times more, then 55th row again. Cut off D and E. Cont in A.

68th row Using A, P to end.
69th row K1, *P2 tog tbl, P25, K1, P25, P2 tog, K1, rep from * once more. 109 sts.
70th row P1, *K26, P1, rep from * 3 times more.
71st row K1, *P2 tog tbl, P23, Pfb, K1, Pfb, P23, P2 tog, K1, rep from * once more.
Rep last 2 rows 4 times more, then 70th row again.
81st row K1, *P2 tog tbl, P24, K1, P24, P2 tog, K1, rep from * once more. 105 sts.
82nd row P to end.
83rd row Using B and C and working in patt from chart (adjusting it as explained on last patt panel), K1, *sl 1, K1, psso, K23, M1, K1, M1, K23, K2 tog, K1, rep from * once more.
84th row Working in patt from chart, P to end.
Rep last 2 rows 5 times more, then 83rd row again. Cut off B and C. Cont in A.
96th row P to end.
97th row K1, *P2 tog tbl, P23, K1, P23, P2 tog, K1, rep from * once more. 101 sts.
98th row P1, *K24, P1, rep from * 3 times more.
99th row K1, P2 tog tbl, P18, turn.
100th and foll 3 alternate rows K to last st, P1.
101st row K1, P2 tog tbl, P13, turn.
103rd row K1, P2 tog tbl, P8, turn.
105th row K1, P2 tog tbl, P3, turn.
107th row K1, P20, K1, P22, P2 tog, K1, P2 tog tbl, P18, turn.
108th row K19, P1, K19, turn.
109th row P17, P2 tog, K1, P2 tog tbl, P13, turn.
110th row K14, P1, K14, turn.
111th row P12, P2 tog, K1, P2 tog tbl, P8, turn.
112th row K9, P1, K9, turn.
113th row P7, P2 tog, K1, P2 tog tbl, P3, turn.
114th row K4, P1, K4, turn.
115th row P4, K1, P20, K1, P to last 3 sts, P2 tog, K1.
116th row P1, K19, turn.
117th and foll 2 alternate rows P to last 3 sts, P2 tog, K1.
118th row P1, K14, turn.
120th row P1, K9, turn.
122nd row P1, K4, turn.
123rd row P4, K1.
124th row P1, *K20, P1, rep from * 3 times more. 85 sts.
125th row Pfb, P5, *(K into front and back of next st—called Kfb—, P4) 3 times, put needle behind first st, K into back of 2nd st, then K first st and sl both sts off tog—called Tw2K—, P4, rep from * twice more, (Kfb, P4) twice, Kfb, P3, Pfb, P1. 99 sts.
126th row K7, P 2nd st, then first st and sl both sts off tog—called Tw2P—, *K4, Tw2P, rep from * to last 6 sts, K6.
127th row P7, Tw2K, *P4, Tw2K, rep from * to last 6 sts, P6.
Rep last 2 rows once more, then 126th row again.

Shape armholes
Bind off 3 sts at beg of next 2 rows. 93 sts.
1st row P2 tog, P2, Tw2K, patt to last 2 sts, P2 tog.
2nd and every alternate row Patt to end.
3rd row P2 tog, P1, Tw2K, patt to last 2 sts, P2 tog.
5th row P3 tog, P5, Tw2K, patt to last 7 sts, P4, P3 tog.
7th row P2 tog, P4, Tw2K, patt to last 2 sts, P2 tog.
9th row P2 tog, P3, Tw2K, patt to last 2 sts, P2 tog.
10th row As 2nd.
Rep last 10 rows 3 times more. Bind off rem 45 sts in patt.

Left front
Using No. 3 (3¼mm) needles and A, cast on 49 sts. Beg with a P row, work 1½in (4cm) reverse stockinette st; end with a K row. Change to No. 6 (4½mm) needles.
Next row K1, *K23, K1, rep from * once.
Next row P1, *K23, P1, rep from * once.
Rep these 2 rows for 1½in (4cm); end with a 2nd row.
Next row K1, P23, K1, P19, turn.
Rep from ** to ** as for back.
Next row P3, Pfb, K1, Pfb, P27, K1.
Next row P to end. 61 sts.
Next row Using B and C and working in patt from chart, K1, sl 1, K1, psso, K27, M1, K1, M1, K27, K2 tog, K1.
Cont working in patt and shaping to match half of back from 28th to 106th row.
Next row K1, P20, K1, P to last 3 sts, P2 tog, K1.
Work 116th to 124th rows as back. ***
Next row Pfb, P5, (Kfb, P4) 3 times, Tw2K, P4, (Kfb, P4) 3 times, P1. 50 sts.
Next row K6, *Tw2P, K4, rep from * to last 2 sts, K2.
Next row P7, Tw2K, *P4, Tw2K, rep from * to last 5 sts, P5.
Work 3 more rows patt as set.

Shape armhole
Bind off 3 sts at beg of next row. Work 1 row. Dec at armhole edge to match back (i.e. dec 6 sts in 10 rows) until 31 sts rem; end with a RS row.

Shape neck
Cont to dec at armhole edge as before, **at same time** bind off 10 sts at beg of next row, 3 sts at beg of foll alternate row, then 2 sts at beg of foll 2 alternate rows. Dec one st at neck edge on next and foll 3 alternate rows; end with a WS row. Bind off rem 2 sts.

Right front
Work as for left front to ***.
Next row P6, (Kfb, P4) 3 times, Tw2K, (P4, Kfb) 3 times, P3, Pfb, P1. 50 sts.
Next row K7, *Tw2P, K4, rep from * to last st, K1.
Cont to match left front, reversing shaping.

Sleeves
Using No 3 (3¼mm) needles and A, cast on 34 sts. Beg with a P row, work 1½in (4cm) reverse stockinette st; end with a K row.
Change to No. 6 (4½mm) needles.
1st row P2, *Kfb, P9, rep from * twice more, Kfb, P1.
2nd row K2, *Tw2P, K9, rep from * twice more, Tw2P, K1.
3rd row P2, *Tw2K, P9, rep from * twice more, Tw2K, P1.
Rep 2nd and 3rd rows throughout, inc one st at each end of 7th row (from beg of patt) and every foll 6th row, working extra sts into reverse stockinette st, until there are 58 sts. Cont straight until sleeve measures 11in (28cm) from hemline (beg of patt); end with a WS row.
Next row P7, Kfb, *P4, Tw2K, P4, Kfb, rep from * 3 times more, P6. 63 sts.
Next row K7, Tw2P, *K4, Tw2P, rep from * to last 6 sts, K6.
Next row P7, Tw2K, *P4, Tw2K, rep from * to last 6 sts, P6.
Rep last 2 rows once more, then first of them again.

Shape top
Bind off 3 sts at beg of next 2 rows. 57 sts.
Rep 10 rows of back armhole shaping 4 times.
Bind off rem 9 sts in patt.

Hood
Using No. 6 (4½mm) needles and A, cast on 89 sts.
1st row P6, Tw2K, (P4, Tw2K) twice, P24, K1, P25, (Tw2K, P4) 3 times, P1.

2nd row
K6, Tw2P, (K4, Tw2P) twice, K24, P1, K25, (Tw2P, K4) 3 times, K1.
Rep these 2 rows for 11¾in (30cm). Bind off.

Hood trim
Using No. 3 (3¼mm) needles and A, cast on 121 sts. K 2 rows.
3rd row
K1, *insert needle into next st, wind yarn twice over point of needle and finger, then over needle again, draw the 3 loops through the st but do not sl the st off needle, put the 3 loops on left-hand needle and K tbl tog with the st—called loop 1 (L1)—, K1, rep from * to end.
K 3 rows.
7th row
K2, *L1, K1, rep from * to last st, K1.
K 2 rows. Bind off.

Front edges
Using No. 3 (3¼mm) needles, A and with RS facing, pick up and K about 90 sts along front edge between hemline and neck edge.
Bind off knitwise.

To finish
Press or block according to yarn used. Join raglan, side and sleeve seams. Turn hems to WS and slip stitch in place. Join top edge of hood. Sew loopy trim inside front edge and sew hood to neck. Sew on toggles in 3 pairs and make loops to fasten them.

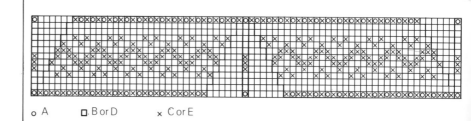

o A   □ B or D   × C or E

SEWING

un at the fair

verals are fun to wear any
me, and aren't difficult to
ake. If you are inexperienced,
n't use bulky fabrics.

Measurements

To fit sizes 10-12[12-14].
Note: Measurements are given for sizes 10 and 12. Measurements for the larger size are given in brackets []. If only one figure is given it applies to both sizes.

Suggested fabrics

The overalls may be made in any fabric commonly used for pants: denim, cotton drill, canvas, velvet, velveteen, pinwale or regular corduroy, flannel, etc.

Materials

$2\frac{3}{4}$[$3\frac{1}{4}$]yd (2.5cm [2.9m]) of 36in (90cm)-wide fabric
Eight $\frac{5}{8}$in (1.5cm)-diameter buttons
2 overall clasps
Matching sewing thread
$\frac{1}{4}$yd (.2m) of 36in (90cm)-wide lining (optional)

Note: $\frac{5}{8}$in (1.5cm) seam allowances have been included throughout. Finish seams with zig zag stitching or overcasting.

1 Following the measurement diagram and cutting layout, cut out two front leg sections, two back leg sections, one front bib, two back bibs, two pockets, two placket strips and four waistbands (two outer sections and two facing sections). One pocket piece and two waistband facings may be cut from lining. The pants sections are easier to cut out if you make a paper pattern first.

2 Place two pocket pieces together, with right sides facing and raw edges matching. Pin, baste and stitch around edges, leaving an opening as shown. Trim seams, clip curves and turn right side out. Press. Slip stitch opening edges. Topstitch twice along upper edge.

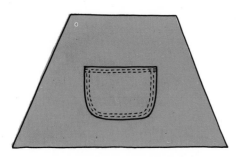

3 Position pocket in the middle of the right side of front bib. Pin and baste in place. Topstitch twice around side and lower edges, stitching $\frac{1}{8}$in (3mm) and $\frac{1}{4}$in (6mm) from edge of pocket.

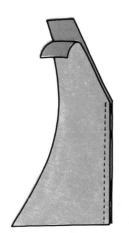

4 Join back bib sections down center back, starting the seam $\frac{5}{8}$in (1.5cm) from top of straight edge. Clip corners.

5 Turn under and baste a $\frac{1}{4}$in (6mm) hem, then a further $\frac{3}{8}$in (1cm) hem down side edges and across top of front bib. Topstitch twice around side and upper edges, $\frac{1}{8}$in (3mm) and $\frac{1}{4}$in (6mm) from edge. Repeat around back bib.

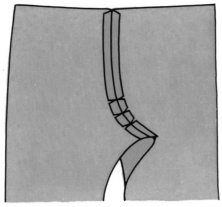

6 Join the two front leg sections, right sides together and raw edges matching, stitching down center front. Repeat for back leg sections. Clip curves.
7 With right sides together and raw edges matching, pin, baste and stitch inside leg seams.

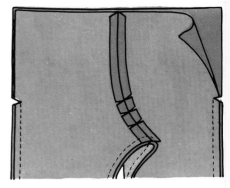

8 Pin, baste and stitch outside leg seams, starting $5\frac{1}{2}$in (14cm) from waist edge. Clip into side seam allowances at the top almost to the stitching.
9 Following the Technique Tip, make a wrap opening on each side, stitching and pressing the wrap inside as shown.

10 Following the pleating diagram, pin and baste pleats across top edge of pants both at the front and the back.

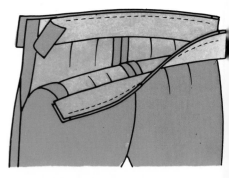

11 Pin and baste one waistband piece to front of pants section, right sides together and raw edges matching. Position waistband facing on the wrong side of the front pants section, right side of facing to wrong side of pants section, thus enclosing the placket facing. Pin and baste in place. Stitch through all three layers. Repeat for back.
12 With right side of front bib matching right side of waistband top edge, pin, baste and stitch bib to waistband. Clip corners of waistband and facing and trim seam allowances. Turn under seam allowance all around free edges of facing and across ends of waistband.

Measurement diagram

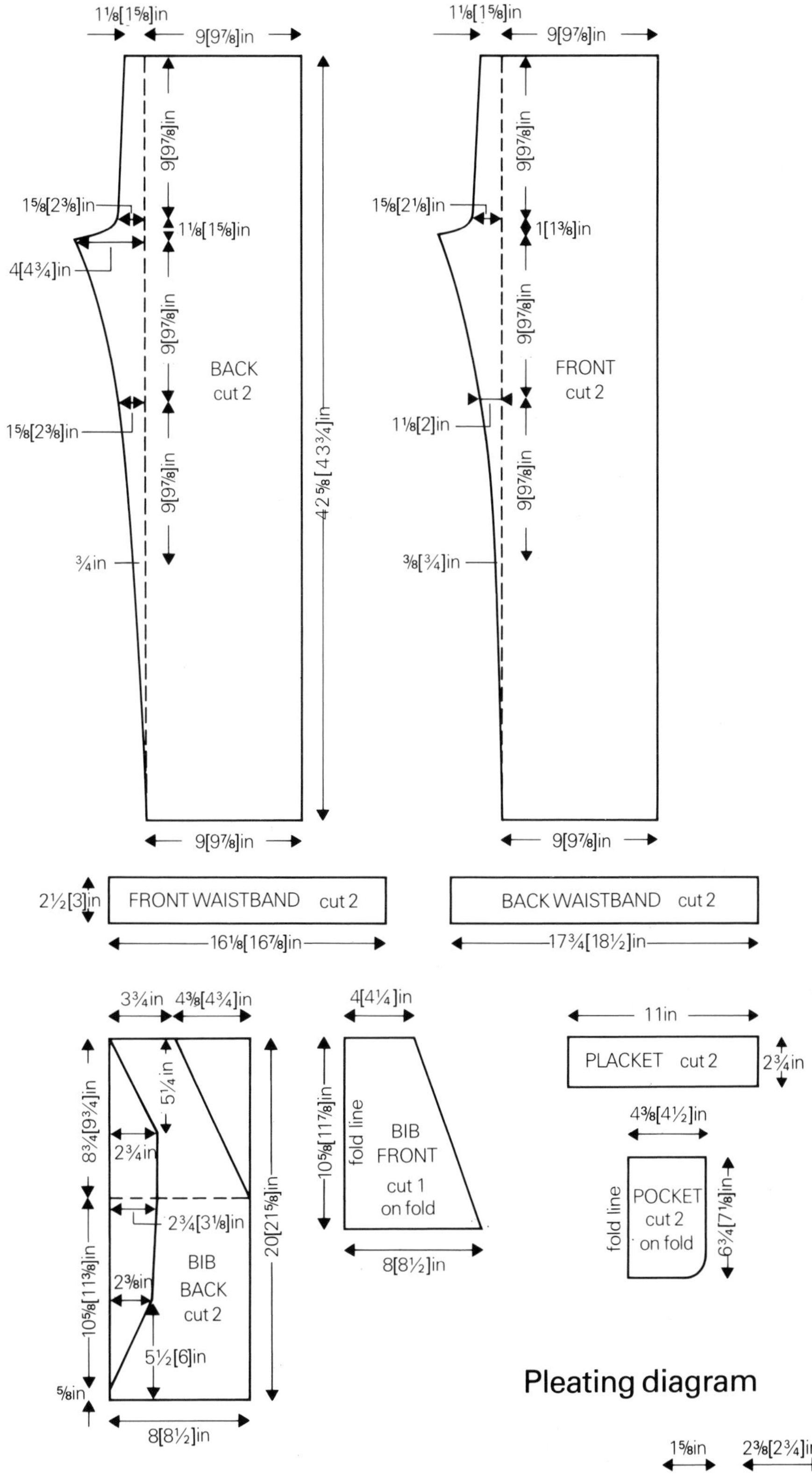

1⅛[1⅝]in
9[9⅞]in
9[9⅞]in
1⅝[2⅜]in
1⅛[1⅝]in
4[4¾]in
9[9⅞]in
BACK
cut 2
1⅝[2⅜]in
9[9⅞]in
¾in
42⅝[43¾]in
9[9⅞]in
1⅛[1⅝]in
9[9⅞]in
9[9⅞]in
1⅝[2⅛]in
1[1⅜]in
9[9⅞]in
FRONT
cut 2
1⅛[2]in
9[9⅞]in
⅜[¾]in
9[9⅞]in
2½[3]in
FRONT WAISTBAND cut 2
16⅛[16⅞]in
BACK WAISTBAND cut 2
17¾[18½]in
3¾in
4⅜[4¾]in
5¼in
8¾[9¾]in
2¾in
2¾[3⅛]in
BIB
BACK
cut 2
10⅝[11⅜]in
2⅜in
20[21⅝]in
5½[6]in
⅝in
8[8½]in
4[4¼]in
10⅝[11⅞]in
fold line
BIB
FRONT
cut 1
on fold
8[8½]in
11in
PLACKET cut 2
2¾in
4⅜[4½]in
fold line
POCKET
cut 2
on fold
6¾[7⅛]in

Cutting layout

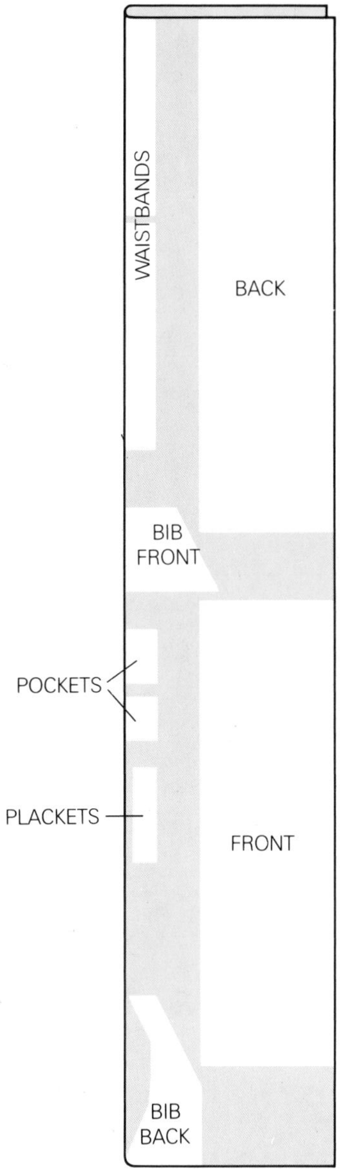

WAISTBANDS
BACK
BIB
FRONT
POCKETS
PLACKETS
FRONT
BIB
BACK

Pleating diagram

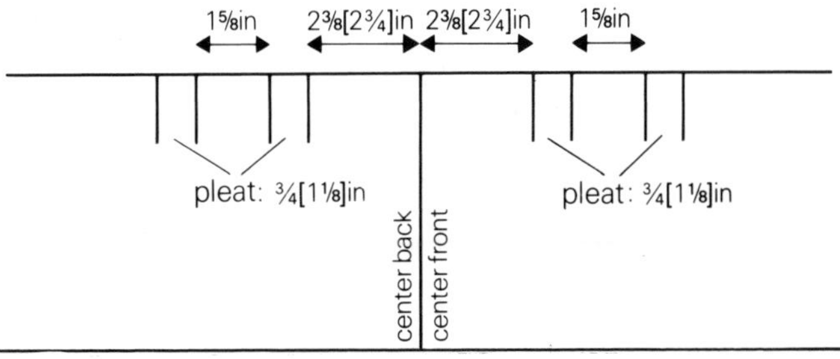

1⅝in
2⅜[2¾]in
2⅜[2¾]in
1⅝in
pleat: ¾[1⅛]in
pleat: ¾[1⅛]in
center back
center front

Brian Mayor

Technique tip

Wrap opening in a seam

This is a useful way of finishing an opening in a side seam where there is no extra fabric for this purpose. The existing seam allowances are simply bound with a strip of fabric.

The placket can be made any width: cut the binding strip to twice the desired finished width, plus $1\frac{1}{4}$in (3cm) for seam allowances. Then clip into seam allowances at the base of the opening

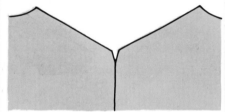

Spread the opening edges so that the seam allowances down the opening are more or less horizontal.

Pin, baste and stitch placket to opening, right sides together and raw edges matching.

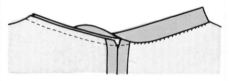

Press under $\frac{5}{8}$in (1.5cm) seam allowance down free edge of binding. Fold the strip over the seam allowances; baste in place. Binding should now be desired width. Slip stitch folded edge of placket to wrong side of opening, following the line of machine stitching.

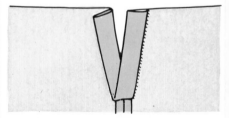

Fold placket at base so that the front of the opening folds back, and the back of the opening lies under the front. Topstitch front placket to front of opening if you like. Stitching across the base of the placket adds strength.

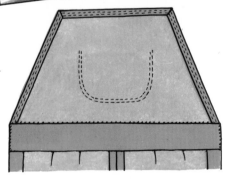

13 Slip stitch long edge of waistband facing to inside of front bib, following stitching line. Slip stitch ends of waistband to facing. Topstitch all around waistband.

14 Repeat steps 12 and 13 to join the back bib and waistband.

15 Try on overalls, pinning straps to front bib temporarily. Mark hems and positions for buttons and buttonholes, positioning one at the waist on each side and two at equal intervals down each side opening.

16 Make buttonholes, and sew on buttons to match.

Sew buttons to top of front bib and attach clasps to straps.

17 Turn up hems and sew by hand.

EXTRA SPECIAL SEWING

One for the road

Get out for some exercise in this comfortable track suit.

Measurements
To fit sizes 10-12 [14-16].
Finished back length of jacket excluding ribbing: $22\frac{1}{2}$in (57cm). Finished side length of pants from waistline excluding ribbing: $40\frac{3}{4}$in (103.5cm).
Note: Measurements are given for size 10-12. Figures for size 14-16 are given in brackets []; If only one figure is given, it applies to all sizes. $\frac{5}{8}$in (1.5cm) seam allowances are included and $\frac{3}{4}$in (2cm) hem for hood casing; $1\frac{5}{8}$in (4cm) hem for waist casing.

Suggested fabrics
Stretch fabrics such as stretch terrycloth, stretch velour, knits.

Materials
$4\frac{7}{8}$yd (4.4m) of 36in (90cm)-wide fabric or 3yd (2.7m) of 60in (150cm)-wide fabric
Matching thread
22in (56cm) open-ended zipper
$2\frac{1}{8}$yd (1.9m) of 2in (5cm)-wide elasticized ribbing or belting
$\frac{7}{8}$yd (.8m) of 1in (2.5cm) elastic
$1\frac{3}{8}$yd (1.2m) of cord for hood drawstring
Yardstick, flexible curve, pencil

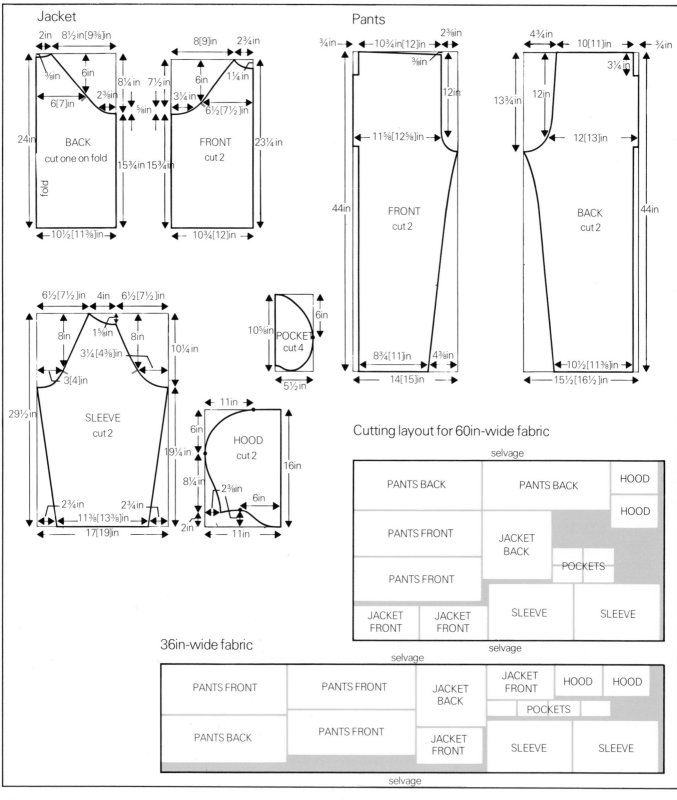

Jacket

BACK cut one on fold

FRONT cut 2

SLEEVE cut 2

POCKET cut 4

HOOD cut 2

Pants

FRONT cut 2

BACK cut 2

Cutting layout for 60in-wide fabric

selvage

PANTS BACK	PANTS BACK	HOOD
PANTS FRONT	JACKET BACK	HOOD
PANTS FRONT		POCKETS
JACKET FRONT / JACKET FRONT	SLEEVE	SLEEVE

selvage

36in-wide fabric

selvage

| PANTS FRONT | PANTS FRONT | JACKET BACK | JACKET FRONT | HOOD | HOOD |
| PANTS BACK | PANTS FRONT | JACKET FRONT | POCKETS | SLEEVE | SLEEVE |

selvage

Cutting out

1 For an accurate fit it is advisable to make a paper pattern for your size first, following the measurement diagram. Check that side seams are the same length on jacket front and back and that the notches correspond on jacket and sleeve. Check that the inner and outer pants seams are the same length, and

adjust the length if necessary before cutting out. Remember to adjust fabric allowance if you lengthen or shorten the pattern.

2 Following the appropriate cutting layout, cut out all the pieces. Remember to place jacket back on a fold and to reverse all remaining pattern pieces when cutting for the second time so that you cut a right and left sleeve, front, etc.

For pockets cut two right pockets and two left.

3 Mark notches on front, back and sleeve with tailor's tacks, or cut them as you cut out the fabric (see Technique Tip).

4 Cut a piece of elastic ribbing to fit just below waistline plus $1\frac{1}{4}$in (3cm) seam allowances. Cut two pieces of elastic ribbing to fit around wrists and two for ankles, allowing $1\frac{1}{4}$in (3cm) extra.

Jacket

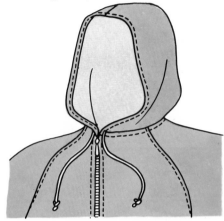

1 With right sides together, pin, baste and stitch sleeves to each armhole edge of fronts and back, matching notches on seams. Trim seam allowances to $\frac{3}{8}$in (1cm), finish and press away from sleeve. Working from right side, topstitch $\frac{1}{4}$in (5mm) away from each armhole seam.

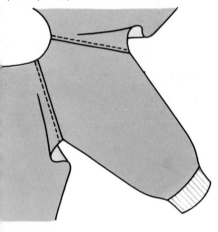

2 With right sides together, pin, baste and stitch wrist elastic to lower edges of sleeves, stretching the elastic to fit the fabric as you work. Trim the seam allowances even with edges of elastic and finish them together.

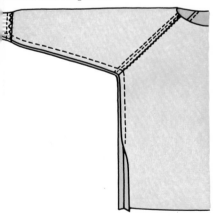

3 With right sides together, pin, baste and stitch side seams of jacket and sleeve in one operation, stitching through elastic at wrist to join the cuff. Press seam open and finish it.

4 With right sides together, pin, baste and stitch waist elastic to lower edge of jacket. This is easier if you divide the elastic into equal sections, allowing $\frac{5}{8}$in (1.5cm) for turning under at each end. Match center of elastic to center back and other dividing marks to seamlines at sides. Pin in place, then machine stitch with the elastic side up, stretching it as you stitch.

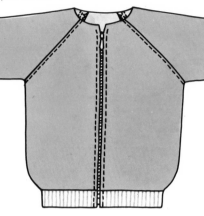

5 Press under $\frac{5}{8}$in (1.5cm) seam allowances down center front of jacket and elastic and finish. Insert zipper, positioning bottom stop at lower edge of ribbing and top stop just below neckline.

6 With right sides together, pin, baste and stitch the two hood sections together around outer curved edge. Trim allowances to $\frac{3}{8}$in (1cm). Finish and press to one side. Working from the right side, topstitch $\frac{1}{4}$in (5mm) away from seam.

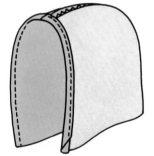

7 Around straight edge of hood, turn under $\frac{1}{4}$in (5mm) and press. Turn under another $\frac{5}{8}$in (1.5cm) and press. Fold under a triangle at neck edge to form a gap for cord to be threaded through later; baste. Stitch close to folded edge, continuing stitching in a straight line over folded triangle to edge of fabric.

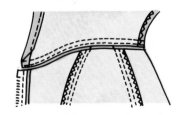

8 With right sides together, pin hood to jacket with folded edges even at center

fronts and center backs matching, easing the hood slightly to fit the jacket. Baste and stitch. Trim jacket seam allowances to $\frac{1}{4}$in (5mm). Press seam toward jacket and fold hood seam allowances over to enclose raw edges. Topstitch close to the fold.

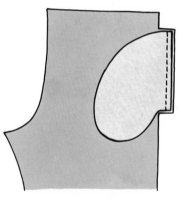

9 Thread cord through hood casing and knot the ends.

Pants

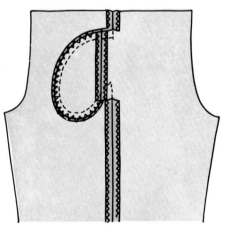

1 With right sides together, pin, baste and stitch pockets to extensions of each pants section at side seams. Trim allowances, finish and press seam open.

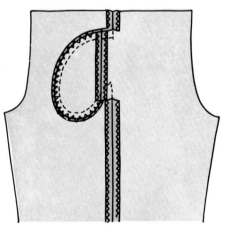

2 With right sides together, pin, baste and stitch fronts to backs at side seams, leaving a 7in (18cm) gap for pocket. Stitch around outer edges of pockets. Snip back seam allowances above and below pocket extensions. Press pocket toward front of pants and press remaining seam open.

3 With right sides together, pin, baste and stitch ankle elastic to lower edge of pants, stretching the elastic to fit the fabric. Trim seam allowances even with the edge of the elastic and finish the two edges together.

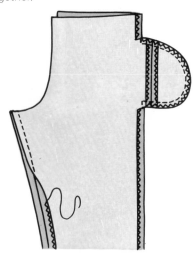

4 Pin, baste and stitch fronts to backs at inside leg seam, continuing stitching through ribbing. Press seam open and finish.

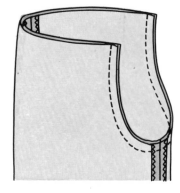

5 Turn one leg right side out and slip it inside the other leg. With right sides together and inside leg seams matching, pin, baste and stitch the crotch seam, leaving a $1\frac{1}{4}$in (3cm) gap $\frac{3}{8}$in (1cm) below top edge on back only.

6 To make casing for elastic, turn under $\frac{3}{8}$in (1cm) along top of pants and press. Turn under another $1\frac{1}{4}$in (3cm) and baste. Stitch close to first folded edge, leaving an opening through which to thread the elastic.

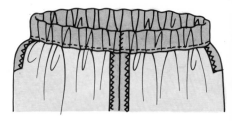

7 Cut elastic to fit waist plus 1in (2.5cm). Insert through opening in casing. Overlap ends by 1in (2.5cm) and sew securely. Slip stitch opening in casing neatly by hand.

Technique tip

Notches

Notches are usually included on paper patterns to make it easier to match seamlines. There is no reason why you cannot mark them yourself when you are cutting your own patterns. They are particularly useful on patterns for garments with curved seams or cutting lines which do not follow the straight grain, like the raglan sleeve seams on the track suit.

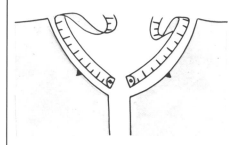

Once you have cut out the pattern, measure the length of the seamlines and check that all seamlines to be joined are the same length. It is important to measure the seamline, not the cutting line.
The measurement diagrams indicate where the notches should be marked.

Once you have cut the pattern, make sure that the straight sections of the seamlines to be joined match, then mark the notches equidistant down the seamline. The remainder of the seamlines should match also, but you may find that, to get an accurate fit, it is necessary to ease one of the sections to the other when pinning and basting.

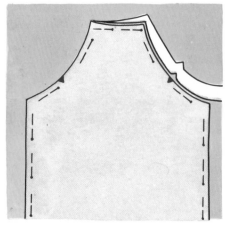

When you cut out the fabric, follow the cutting line, but at the points where the notches are, cut a little notch in the fabric, out from the cutting line.

When you pin and baste the sleeves, match the notches to those on the bodice as you work.

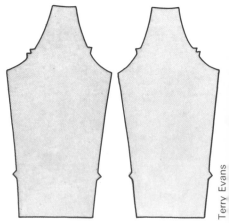

Terry Evans

It is often helpful to vary the number of notches in order to indicate which pattern pieces correspond. For example, on the raglan sleeves you may find it helpful to mark a single notch on the front and the front seam of the sleeve and a double notch on the back and the back seam of the sleeve. Then there is no danger that you will join the front sleeve seam to the back or vice versa.

Homemaker

Boys and girls together . . .

. . . dance across these cross-stitched café curtains. You can repeat the motif as many times as you like to suit the width of your window. Use either a pleated or a plain, gathered heading.

Ron Kelly/Designed by Gisela Banbury

Finished size: The directions are for two curtains, each 59in (150cm) wide, unpleated, and 42in (107cm) long.

Materials
5½yd (5m) of 32in (80cm)-wide evenweave cotton with 26 threads to 1in (2.5cm)*
35 skeins of stranded embroidery floss
Small tapestry needle
3½yd (3.1m) of drapery pleater tape and hooks (optional)
Matching sewing thread

*Note: If you use evenweave with a different number of threads to 1in (2.5cm), you will need to calculate the number of threads covered by each motif before buying your fabric. Each complete motif goes across 320 vertical threads, with each stitch worked over 4 threads. If your fabric is finer or coarser than ours you can keep the motifs approximately the same size by working the stitches over more or fewer threads respectively. Once you have decided on the number of threads per stitch, multiply this by 75 – the number of squares across the motif – to get the number of threads per complete motif. Divide this by the number of threads per 1in (2.5cm) in your fabric to get the width of each complete motif. Use this figure as a guide in planning the number of motifs you will need on each curtain panel and their positioning. You may need to adjust the fabric requirements to obtain the correct width. Our curtains have an individual boy or girl at each side, but you can begin and end with complete motifs.

1 Cut the fabric into four equal lengths. Finish all raw edges (not selvages) with overcasting or zig-zag stitch. Trim off the selvages and join two of the lengths along these edges with French seams. Repeat with the remaining two lengths. You now have two panels, each approximately 49in (125cm) long and 62in (155cm) wide.
2 If you are using pleater tape, cut a piece a little longer than the width of one curtain panel, place it along the upper edge and plan the positions of the pleats. Mark the finished side edges – that is, the fold line for the side hems – with basting, taking the basting all the way down to the lower edge, following the grain of the fabric. Repeat on the other curtain panel. Do not apply the tape yet. If you are using a simple casing, there is no need to mark the side hems.
3 Begin the embroidery with the diamond border. Measure up 6in (15cm) from the

lower edge and 1¼in (3cm) (or a little more than the depth of the side hem) from the left-hand edge of the right-hand curtain. Begin at this point with the widest part of each diamond, using the tapestry needle and all six strands of the floss. Work the diamonds all the way across the curtain, finishing (preferably with a complete diamond) the same distance as before from the side edge.
4 Still working on the right-hand curtain and still using six strands of floss, work the figure motifs. Start at the left-hand edge, 12 horizontal threads above the top of the diamonds and about 2in (5cm) from the edge of the fabric and work the individual boy motif, beginning at the point shown on the chart. (Or begin with a complete motif, if appropriate for your fabric and curtain width.) Now work complete motifs across the width of the curtain, finishing with an individual girl motif, placed 2in (5cm) from the right-hand edge.
5 Work the embroidery on the left-hand curtain, beginning as before with the diamond border and then working the figure motifs, starting at the inner edge with the individual girl motif and finishing with a boy motif at the outer edge.
6 Press the embroidery on the wrong side, using a hot iron over a damp cloth.
7 If you are using pleater tape, apply it to the upper edge of each curtain, following the manufacturer's instructions.
8 Turn under ¼in (5mm) along the side edges and press. Turn under the side hems along the lines of basting and baste them in place. Hem by hand.
9 If you are using a casing as a heading, measure from a point 2½in (6.5cm) below the diamond border up to the desired finished upper edge. Mark this with a line of basting. Measure the thickness of the curtain rod, add 1in (2.5cm) and trim the fabric to leave a margin of this measurement above the basted line. Turn under and press ⅜in (1cm) along the raw edge. Fold again along the basted line and baste the casing in place. Machine stitch about ¼in (5mm) from the first fold to complete the casing.
10 Turn under and press ⅜in (1cm) along the lower edge of each curtain. Bring this folded edge up to the center of the diamond border on the wrong side. Baste it in place and hand hem, taking the hemming stitches through the embroidery stitches only, not through the fabric to the right side.
11 Slip stitch the side edges of the lower hems to the side hems, using tiny stitches and mitering the corners.
12 Press the curtains, avoiding the tape, if used.

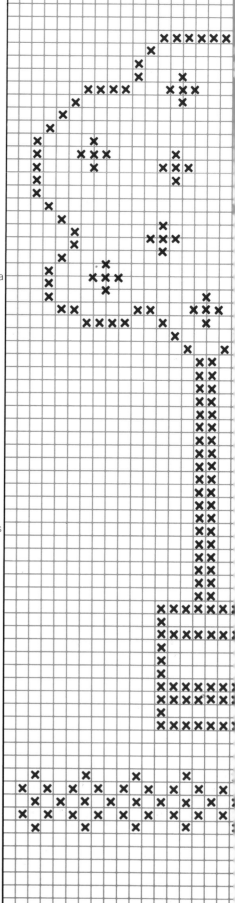

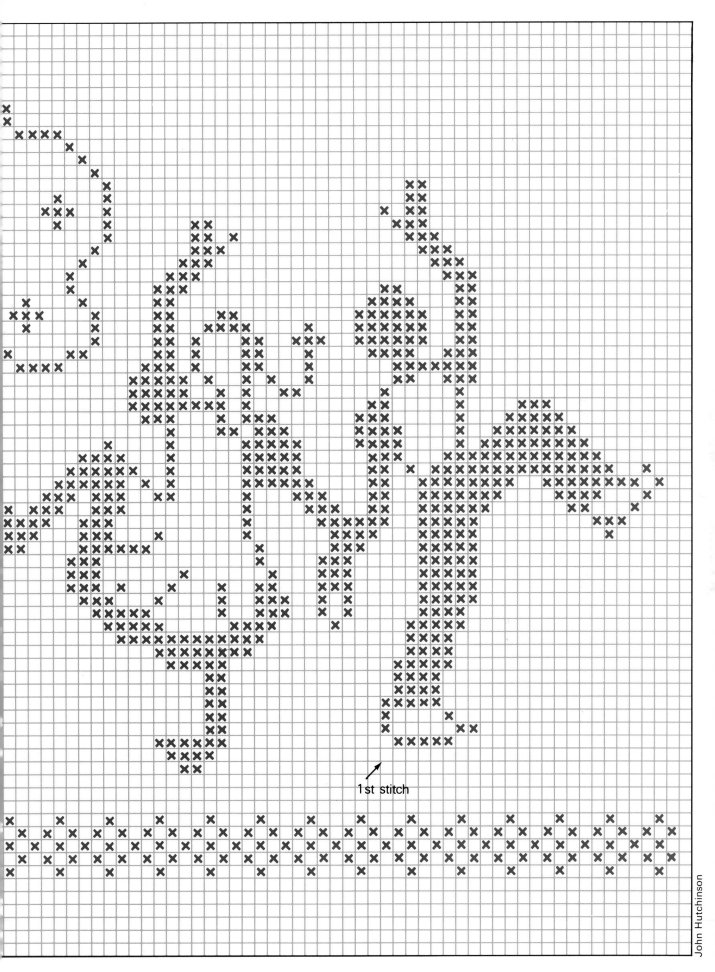

1st stitch

Homemaker

Cover-up story: Slipcovers (1)

Having a chair covered by a professional upholsterer can be expensive. With our easy-to-follow instructions, you can become the expert and give your furniture a real facelift. Here we show how to take measurements, choose the fabric and cut it out.

Skirts

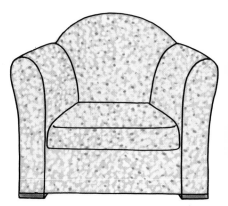

Covers can be finished with a fitted base and simply tied under the chair. For a fitted base, add 6in (15cm) to the length of sides, front and back for a turn-under allowance and for the hem.

Slipcovers are the best way to brighten up a shabby armchair or sofa and, if well made, can make an old piece of furniture look brand new. They also have the practical advantage of being removable for cleaning, so they retain a crisp, clean appearance over many years. Slipcovers are not difficult to make, if you have basic sewing skills, so don't be dismayed by the sheer magnitude of the task. However, you will need plenty of time, patience and a large work area. Here we show you how to measure the furniture and calculate the amount of fabric needed; on pages 116-118 there are step-by-step instructions for constructing the cover.

Preparing the chair

With the exception of those upholstered in leather and plastic, almost any armchair or sofa can be given a new lease on life with slipcovers, but they will not hide lumps, bumps or broken chair springs, so before starting the job, take a good look at the chair you want to cover. If the cushions have lost their shape and the filling has gone limp, consider replacing them. If the furniture is secondhand, scrutinize it for woodworm and treat accordingly. Even if the chair is sound, give it a spring cleaning by vacuuming thoroughly, and if necessary shampoo the upholstery.

Choosing a suitable fabric

Tough, firm, closely-woven fabrics such as chintz or heavy poplin are best for slipcovers. Pick a fabric that is washable or can be dry cleaned, is colorfast and pre-shrunk. If you aren't sure about shrinkage, wash or clean the fabric before cutting out the slipcovers.
Very thick fabrics should be avoided; they are difficult to work with and their bulk on seams makes it almost impossible to achieve a smooth-fitting cover. Fabric design must also be carefully considered. If the design repeat is more

than 24in (61cm), fabric will be wasted matching the design and centering it on cushions, so it is uneconomical. Repeats of 12in (30cm) are more practical but even these can overwhelm a small chair. Remember, bold fabrics will dominate a room, whereas small prints will blend with existing furnishings. Plain fabrics are the easiest and most economical to work with, as there is no matching to do. Check also for nap: velveteen slipcovers, for instance, should always be made with the nap smoothed down.

Finishes

Cording

Cording improves the appearance of a slipcover, but if you have no experience with this sewing method, or if your sewing machine is unable to cope with four thicknesses of fabric, it would be better to make the cover without cording. The best way to calculate the quantities of cord needed is simply to measure the existing seams on the old cover. As a guide, a sofa takes about 43yd (40m) of cord, so allow an extra $2\frac{1}{4}$yd (2m) of fabric for covering the cord. For a chair, allow 22yd (20m) of cord and an extra 1yd (.9m) of fabric.
To pre-shrink new filler cord before use, wind the cord into a hank, then hot

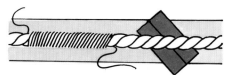

wash and dry as quickly as possible.
To join two pieces of cord, unravel the strands slightly at each end and trim each strand to a different length. Wind the strands together, then bind the joining with thread.
To cover the cord, cut out $1\frac{1}{4}$in (3cm) wide bias strips of fabric. Join fabric strips together diagonally, on the straight grain. Fold fabric around cord, wrong side inside; pin and baste firmly in place.

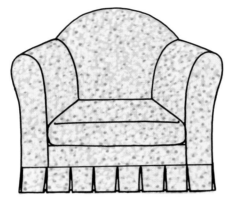

sides and add 14in (36cm) to each measurement for corner pleats.

figure by three, adding ¾in (2cm) for seam allowances.

Measuring the chair

When measuring for and making the cover, work to the existing seamlines on the original upholstery.

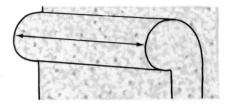

A plain skirt, with box pleats at each corner, can be added to the cover. Skirts are usually 6in (15cm) deep. To calculate the fabric needed for a plain skirt, decide on the depth and add 4in (10cm) for seam allowances and hem. Measure around the chair back, front and

Another finish is a skirt with box pleats or a gathered flounce. The depth of the skirt will be the same as for the plain skirt. Measure around chair; multiply the

On scroll armchairs there will be an additional seam across the outside arm to improve the fit of the cover. Always take the measurements at the widest part of the chair.

Add 1½in (4cm) to each measurement for a ¾in (2cm) seam allowance.

The 4in (10cm) tuck-in allowance is for the extra fabric that is tucked in between the chair back, arms and seat to hold the cover firmly in place.

For a cover with a fitted base, remember to add 6in (15cm) to the length measurements of sides, front and back. For rectangular cushions, measure the top, base and sides and add on seam allowance. For shaped cushions, measure the top and base at the widest parts and cut out rectangles; these can be trimmed to fit the cushion when pinned together.

Calculating the amount of fabric

Each chair or sofa must be measured and fabric requirements calculated individually. However as a rough indication of quantities, if you use 48in (122cm)-wide fabric, you will need about 24yd (22m) for a sofa and two armchairs; for an armchair, about 7½yd (7m). After measuring the chair (see right), check measurements and appropriate allowances for seams, tuck-in and turn-under at base. Include measurements for cushions and a skirt, if required.

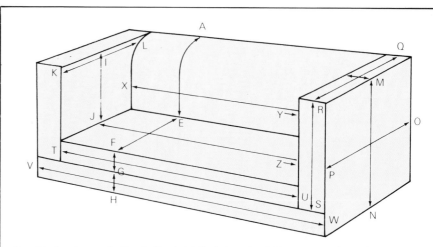

Outside back	A–B	C–D	Add 6in (15cm) to B for turn-under at base
Inside back	A–E	X–Y	Add 4in (10cm) "tuck-in" allowance to E, X & Y
Seat	E–F	J–Z	Add 4in (10cm) "tuck-in" allowance to E, J & Z
Seat front	F–G	T–U	A tuck-in allowance may need to be added to T & U
Lower seat front	G–H	V–W	Add 6in (15cm) to H for turn-under at base
Outside arm	M–N	P–O	Add 6in (15cm) to N for turn-under at base
Inside arm	I–J	K–L	Add 4in (10cm) "tuck-in" allowance to L & J
Arm top	I–M	Q–R	
Arm front	I–M	R–S	
Cushion pieces			
Skirt	See Finishes on page 112.		

John Hutchinson

Elizabeth Whiting

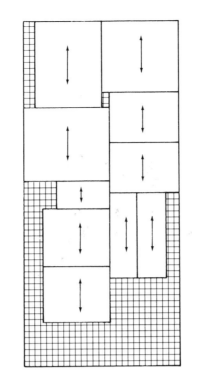

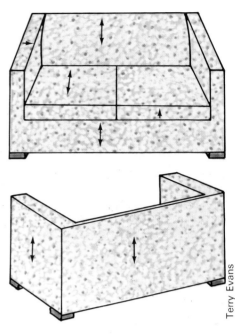

The diagrams above indicate which way the grain should run on each peice.

Next make a layout chart. Draw this to scale $\frac{1}{8}$in = 1in (or 1mm = 1cm) on graph paper. On the graph paper draw an elongated rectangle with the width corresponding to that of the fabric—for example, 6in for 48in (or 12.2cm for 122cm)-wide fabric. If the fabric has been chosen, mark any repeat to scale along the graph representation. On a sheet of plain paper draw and cut out your pattern pieces to the same scale. On each one mark the top and what it represents. Position the pattern pieces on the graph paper layout and move them around to get the most economical layout. On the layout, make sure that the grain lines run in the same direction and that the design motifs are centered. Allow the fabric for the cording, if seams are to be corded.

Pin all the pieces in place and measure the length of the layout. Convert the measurement from inches to yards (or centimeters to meters). This is the amount of fabric you should buy, but be generous rather than skimpy with the fabric. Leftover fabric can always be used for matching throw pillows or for protective arm covers. Keep the layout as a cutting guide.

How to make a slipcover

1 Check the chair's condition and decide if it is worth covering. Make any repairs.

2 Choose your fabric and note the size of the pattern repeats. Do not buy the fabric at this stage.

3 Measure the chair.

4 Draw layout and calculate fabric requirements.

5 Calculate the exact amount of fabric needed, bearing in mind pattern repeats, cording and the finish to the base of the cover.

6 Buy the fabric.

7 Cut out the fabric following the layout.

8 Fit the fabric to the chair, trimming pieces as necessary; pin the cover together.

9 Insert the cording and baste the cover together.

10 Check the fit of the cover; stitch it together.

11 Finish the cover around the base.

Homemaker

Here we complete the course on slipcovers by showing how to fit the cover, finish the base and make the cushions.

Cover-up story: Slipcovers (2)

Cutting out the fabric pieces

1 Check that your paper layout is accurate before cutting out the fabric pieces (see page 115).

2 If you are working with a large fabric design, double check that it will appear in the center of the cushions and, when joining fabric widths to cover the sofa back, make sure that the design matches across the seams.

3 Remember to cut out only simple rectangles. These rectangles will be cut to shape as they are fitted piece by piece onto the chair.

4 As each piece is cut out, mark the top on each one and what part of the chair it will cover.

Fitting

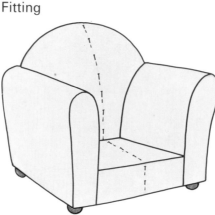

1 Mark a center line with pins or tailor's

chalk down the center back of the chair and its seat.

2 Using bright-colored thread and large basting stitches, mark the center line on each fabric piece along the straight grain. This helps to keep the fabric absolutely straight and gives the cover a more professional-looking fit.

3 The cover is put together inside out on the chair. Work methodically, always pinning, trimming, basting and then stitching.

4 Begin by placing the inside back panel on the chair, matching the basted line on the cover to the pins on the chair and keeping the fabric straight. Smooth out any wrinkles. Pin the inside back panel to the chair to hold it firmly in place.

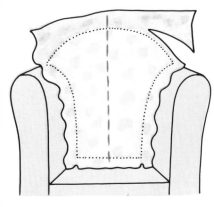

5 Repeat step 4 with the outside back panel, pinning it to the inside back panel along the top seamline. If this seam is curved, the fabric will have to be eased or small darts made to achieve a smooth fit. Trim off any excess fabric to within $\frac{3}{4}$in (2cm) of the pinned fitting line.

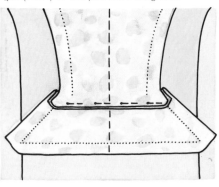

6 Place the seat cover in position with the small seam allowance at the front and the larger tuck-in allowance at the sides and back; fold the tuck-in allowance back on itself.
Pin the inside back panel and seat cover together along the tuck-in allowance.
7 Place the inside, top and outside arm pieces over one chair arm and pin together to fit.
8 The outside arm should also be fitted to the outside back panel and the inside arm to the inside back panel and seat cover. Allow for the tuck-in around seat.

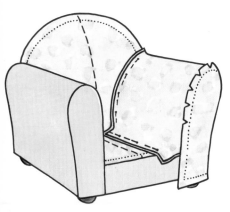

9 Fit the front arm piece. If the seams follow a curve, clip the seam allowance.

10 Repeat steps 7 to 9 to fit the other arm of the chair.
11 Fit the seat front. Depending on the chair design, this piece can be awkward because the side seams at the top may need to be seamed to the tuck-in at the side of the seat, while lower down they are seamed to the front arm piece.
12 If the cover is to have a skirt, leave its fitting until the major part of the cover is completed.
13 If the cover is to be corded, be extra careful that the fitting lines (future seamlines) are clearly marked with either pins or tailor's chalk.
14 Notch the seam allowances so that the pieces can be matched together again easily.
15 To insert cording, first remove the cover from the chair. Unpin each seam, a little at a time, insert the covered cord and re-pin the seam.
16 If the cover is not corded, the pieces need not be taken apart.
17 Baste and stitch any fitting darts.
18 Baste the cover together. Turn the cover right side out. Place the cover, right side out, over the chair. Check the fit of the cover on the chair and make any final adjustments.
19 Remove from chair. Stitch together, leaving a seam open at back corner.

Finishing the base

Fitted base

A slipcover fitted along the lower edge is held in place under the chair by a drawstring of cotton tape. Measure around the lower edge of the chair for the correct tape length.

1 Unpick the base seams to within $\frac{3}{8}$in (1cm) of chair bottom.
2 With cover in place, turn the chair upside down.
3 Pin the fabric around the castors at each of the four corners as shown.
4 Make a $1\frac{1}{4}$in (3.5cm) double casing hem to finish the lower edge of the four flaps and to carry the drawstring; pin in place.
5 Remove the cover; baste and stitch each casing hem in place.

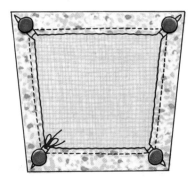

6 Starting at the opening corner, thread the drawstring tape through each casing in turn.

7 Place the cover over the chair. Pull up the drawstring tape to fit and tie the ends together. Do not cut off the excess tape, as the fullness is needed when the cover is removed for cleaning. Tuck the ends up under one of the hems.

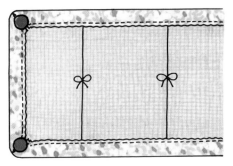

8 If the chair is large or if you are covering a sofa, a combination of a casing tape and tapes tied across the base is best. Simply cut two tapes the depth of the sofa for each tie. Stitch in place under the hem at opposite sides of the cover. Space the ties at about 12in (30cm) intervals along the length of the cover.

Box pleated skirt base

1 Fit the cover on the chair. Measuring from the floor, mark seamline for skirt.
2 If the seam is to be corded, baste the covered cord in place.
3 Pin, baste and stitch the four skirt strips together to make one long strip.

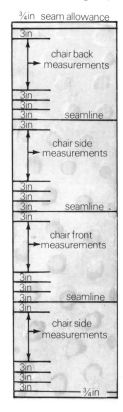

¾in seam allowance
3in
chair back measurements
3in
3in
3in seamline
3in
chair side measurements
3in
3in
3in seamline
3in
chair front measurements
3in
3in
3in seamline
3in
chair side measurements
3in
3in
3in ¾in

4 Measure off 3in (7.5cm) for pleats on each side of each seam as shown. In this way all the seams will be hidden in the finished skirt.

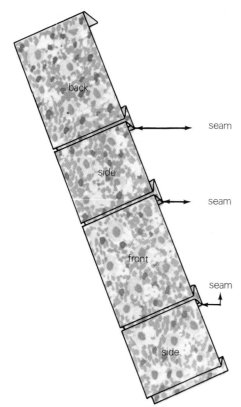

Cushions

1 Plain rectangular cushion covers are stitched together taking a ¾in (2cm) seam allowance.
2 Pin, baste and stitch the ends of the cushion side piece (cushion gusset) together to form a ring.

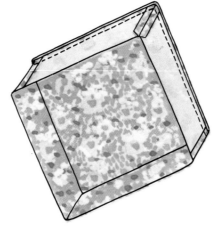

3 Placing right sides together, pin, baste and stitch cushion side piece to all four edges of one cushion piece. If the cushions are corded, insert covered cord between side and cover pieces before stitching them.

4 Match second cushion piece to opposite long edge of side piece with right sides together, inserting cording if used. Pin and baste. Stitch together, starting 2in (5cm) in from one corner on one side and ending 2in (5cm) along at the opposite end of the first side. Clip corners and seam allowances. Turn cushion cover right side out.
5 Finish the opening as for the main cover. Fit over the cushion.
Note: If the cushions are shaped, pin and fit the covers on the cushions as for the main cover.

5 Pleat the fabric following the marks as shown.
6 Baste along the top of the skirt to hold the pleats in place.
7 Remove the cover from the chair. Pin and baste the skirt in place, starting at the open corner.
8 Replace the cover on the chair; check the fit and mark the hemline.
9 Remove the cover. Stitch the skirt to the cover. Turn up a double hem; baste and sew in place by hand.

The opening

The opening down one of the side back seams needs to be finished as neatly as possible and is always left until last to achieve a good fit.

1 Bind the two opening edges with 3in (7.5cm)-wide strips of matching fabric, to finish them.
2 Fasten the opening with hooks and eyes or strips of Velcro®, insert a zipper or simply sew the opening edges together by hand when the cover is finished.

Finishing the cover

1 Trim off any excess seam allowance and press all the seams open.
2 Press the cover well and fit it on the chair. Give the cover a final pressing in place if required.
3 When refitting the cover after cleaning, fit the cover on the chair while it is still damp and again if necessary give it a pressing.

Homemaker

The perfect screen

An old wooden screen becomes an elegant room divider when covered with a bright floral print on one side and contrasting pleated moiré on the other.

Belinda

Finished size

Each panel of this screen measures 62 × 17¾in (158 × 45cm), but the instructions can be adapted to suit most wooden screens.

Materials

4¾yd (4.3m) of 54in (137cm)-wide printed furnishing fabric
7⅝yd (7m) of 48in (122cm)-wide solid-color furnishing fabric
7⅝yd (7m) of 36in (90cm)-wide iron-on interfacing
16yd (14.8m) of filler cord
Matching sewing thread
Transparent tape; graph paper
Tailor's chalk
Upholstery tacks and hammer

1 Remove old fabric from the screen, stripping it down to the wooden frame.
2 Remove all the tacks and nails and unscrew and remove the hinges to separate each panel.
3 From the solid-color fabric cut out four lengths, each 6in (15cm) longer than the height of the screen.

4 On one piece of this fabric mark the guide lines for the pleating. First fold the fabric in half lengthwise, selvages together. Baste along the folded edge to mark the center line.

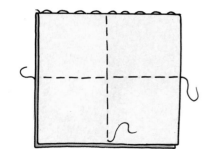

5 Refold the fabric in half widthwise, matching short edges, and baste along the fold. Mark two more lines with basting stitches, halfway between the center line and the short edges. Make sure that these widthwise lines all run parallel and are at right angles to the first lengthwise line.
6 Repeat steps 4 and 5 on each piece of solid-color fabric.

7 Make a pattern for the pleating. Cut out a 2in (5cm)-wide strip of graph paper as long as the fabric is wide. Draw a line across the middle of the strip to mark the center line.

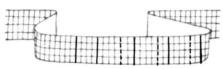

8 On one side, working outward from the center, draw a solid line 1½in (4cm) away, then a broken line 1½in (4cm) away. Draw a second solid line ¾in (2cm) from the broken line and a second broken line 1½in (4cm) away and then a third solid line ¾in (2cm) beyond that. Continue marking the remainder of the strip in broken and solid lines every 1½in (4cm) and ¾in (2cm). Repeat on the opposite side of the center line.

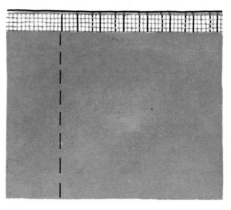

9 Lay one piece of fabric flat with right side up. Position the pleating pattern across one short edge of the fabric, matching the marked center line on the pattern to the basted center line on the fabric. Using tailor's chalk, mark the pleat lines on the fabric just inside the edge. Remove the pattern.
10 Position the pattern again on the fabric at the opposite end of the fabric and again mark the pleats. Remove the pattern.
11 Line up the pattern along each of the widthwise basted lines in turn and repeat the pleat markings.

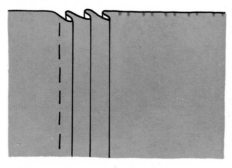

12 Start pleating one side of the fabric, with the mark nearest the center line. Fold the first solid line to meet the first broken line, forming the pleat. Continue

Terry Evans

Belinda

120

to pleat across the fabric in the same way from the top to halfway down the fabric length, using the markings as a guide. Adjust the fabric until it is quite flat. Pin the ends of the pleats together. End the pleating about $1\frac{1}{4}$in (3.5cm) from the selvage edges.

13 On the same side of the fabric, complete the pleating down to the opposite short edge of the fabric, pinning the ends together.

14 Repeat steps 12 and 13, working in the opposite direction from the center. This will result in the formation of a double-size center pleat.

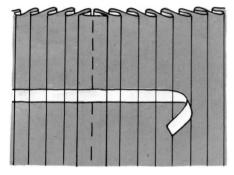

15 Press the fabric. Fasten the pleats temporarily with transparent tape. Baste securely at each end, and across the center.

16 Cut a piece of interfacing the same size as the pleated fabric.

17 Place the shiny side of the interfacing on the wrong side of the pleated fabric, matching all edges. Pin, baste and iron in place.

18 Stitch across top and bottom of pleats just inside the fabric edges.

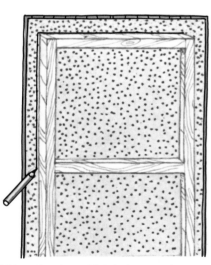

19 Lay the pleated fabric flat, interfaced side up. Mark the center point on the top and bottom of a wooden panel. Lay it on the fabric with center points matching. Draw around the edges of the panel on the interfacing.

20 Repeat steps 9 to 19 to prepare the remaining three solid-color fabric pieces in the same way.

Belinda

21 For printed fabric sides of screen, measure the width and length of a panel and add twice the frame thickness to each measurement, plus $1\frac{1}{4}$in (3cm) for seam allowances.

22 From printed fabric cut out four pieces to this measurement, matching up the design across the four pieces. Mark each panel piece from 1 to 4.

23 From remaining fabric cut 2in (5cm)-wide bias strips and join together on the straight grain for cording. The strip for each panel should measure twice the length of the panel plus the width plus 4in (10cm).

24 Fold the bias strip in half evenly around the cord, wrong sides inside and long edges matching. Pin, baste and stitch down length of cording, close to cord.

25 Place one printed fabric piece right side up and centered over one wooden panel. Pin the excess fabric into darts at the four corners, so that the fabric will fit well. Remove fabric from frame.

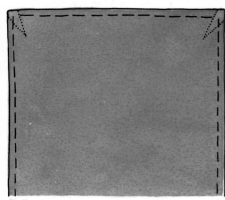

26 Mark the darts. On the wrong side of the fabric, mark the seamline $\frac{5}{8}$in (1.5cm) from the raw edge.
27 Re-pin the darts on the wrong side of the fabric with right sides together. Baste and stitch each dart.

28 Apply the cording around the top and side edges of the printed fabric panel, leaving 2in (5cm) free at each bottom corner. Position the cording along the marked line on the right side of the fabric with raw edges turned outward. Pin, baste and stitch the fabric along the marked line, using a zipper or cording foot. At corners, clip into the seam allowance of the cording fabric.
29 Repeat steps 25 to 28 to prepare the remaining three pieces of printed fabric in the same way.

30 Lay the printed cover pieces 2 and 3 side by side. On each adjoining side, measure and mark the cording halfway between the top and bottom and again 7in (18cm) from top and bottom edges. At each mark unpick the cording from the main fabric until a hinge will fit in the gap. Make sure that the gaps on both cover pieces correspond. To accommodate the hinges, unpick the fabric around the cording and cut away the cord inside. Close the cording fabric and re-stitch it to the main fabric.

31 Placing right sides together, match one pleated fabric piece to one printed fabric piece with marked line on pleated piece to cording line. Pin and baste around three sides, ending 3in (7.5cm) from bottom edge on each side. Check that the cover will fit the appropriate panel. Stitch the pieces together. Trim seam allowances and turn cover right side out.
32 Repeat step 31 to assemble the remaining three panel covers.

33 Slide the first cover over the first wooden panel, easing the darts onto the corners and pulling into shape.
Slip stitch the last 3in (7.5cm) along the bottom of each side.
Cut off the excess cording and tuck in the ends of the fabric neatly.

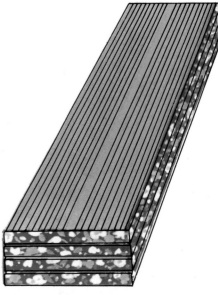

34 At the bottom edge turn under the seam allowance on the printed fabric at the marked line. Tuck raw edges of pleated fabric under this hem. Fix the cover to the wood along the bottom edge with tacks and hammer.

35 Lay the panels over each other in a 1, 2, 3, 4 sequence with like fabrics facing and the top panel with the pleated side up.
36 Fix the middle two panels together with three hinges along the side where the gaps have been cut in the cord, positioning each hinge over a pair of gaps.
37 Join the top two panels together in the same way on the opposite side (away from cording).
38 Finally, join the bottom two panels on the same side as the top two, with the hinges in the same positions.

Terry Evans

123

Homemaker

Jennie and Johnny

These two sweethearts are made from a pair of socks! Their clothes are made from scraps of fabric and their old-fashioned charm will delight any child.

Jennie

Size

About 9½in (24cm) tall.
A seam allowance of ¼in (5mm) has been included throughout.

Materials

One man's plain white cotton sock, size 9–11
Piece of white cotton fabric 10¼×6¼in (26×16cm)
8½in (22cm) of ¼in (5mm)-wide white nylon lace
Piece of blue/white dotted cotton fabric 16×11½in (40×29cm)
Piece of white eyelet lace edging with scalloped edge 8½×3in (22×7.5cm)
14in (36cm) of ⅜in (1cm)-wide woven tape
Piece of white felt 4½×¾in (11×2cm)
Piece of red felt 5½×2in (14×5cm)
One ⅜in (1cm)-diameter red button
10in (25cm) of ¼in (5mm)-wide red ribbon
Gold colored bouclé yarn for hair
Felt-tipped pens and lipstick for features
Stuffing; matching thread
Tracing paper; dressmaker's carbon

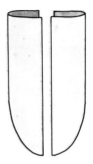

1 For the body cut the toe off the sock across the instep.
2 Fold the sock so that the back of the heel is on the top—this will be the face.

3 Cut up through the middle of the sock from the ankle for about 4in (10cm) to make the legs. Turn the sock wrong side out. Pin, baste and stitch around the slit to form the legs. Trim and turn the body right side out.
4 Stuff the legs. Be careful not to overstuff them, as the fabric is easily stretched out of shape. Pin, baste and stitch across the tops of the legs, so that they will bend.

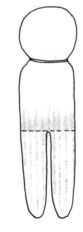

5 Stuff the rest of the body up to the neck. Wind a length of sewing thread around the neck and fasten off.
6 Stuff the head. Again, be careful not to overstuff, so that the head will be the correct shape. Turn in the open edges of the head and slip stitch them together to close.

7 Use the toe part of the sock for the arms. Cut the toe part in half lengthwise. Turn each part wrong side out. Pin, baste and stitch around each part to form an arm, leaving an opening. Turn the arms right side out.

8 Stuff each arm as for legs, step 4, leaving the top of each arm flat. Turn in opening edges and slip stitch them together to close.
9 Sew an arm to each side of the body.
10 Trace pattern pieces for the clothes given on page 127, positioning center of dress on fold of paper.
11 Mark the pattern pieces on the wrong side of the appropriate fabrics the number of times stated. Cut out. Cut out soles and tops of shoes in felt.

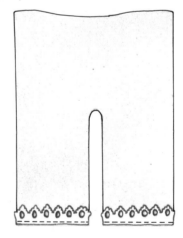

12 Finish the edges of each bloomer leg. Pin, baste and stitch a length of narrow lace to the edge of each leg, matching right side of lace to right side of bloomer fabric.
13 Place bloomer pieces together with right sides facing. Pin, baste and stitch side and inside leg seams, catching in lace. Turn bloomers right side out.

Terri Lawlor

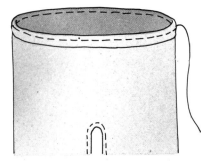

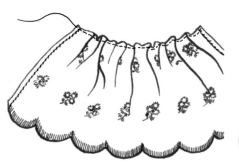

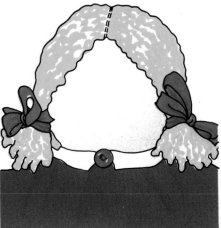

14 Make a $\frac{1}{8}$in (3mm) double hem at waist edge of bloomers. Pin, baste and run a line of gathering stitches around the waist hem. Fit the bloomers over the doll, pull up the gathering stitches around the waist and fasten off securely.

15 Run a line of gathering stitches around the edge of each bloomer leg. Pull up gathering stitches to fit each leg and fasten off securely.

22 Run a line of gathering stitches along the long straight edge of eyelet lace fabric for apron. Pull up gathering to measure $4\frac{1}{4}$in (10.5cm) and fasten off. Turn a $\frac{1}{4}$in (5mm) double hem at each side. Pin, baste and hand-hem.

23 Fold the apron waistband in half lengthwise, edges matching and wrong side inside. Place it over the gathered edge of apron. Pin, baste and stitch in place.

30 Place the hair across the head, slightly in front of the sides and hand-sew to the head, along the center part. Cut red ribbon in half. Draw up the hair into bunches at each side of the face and tie each bunch with a length of red ribbon. Tie ribbon into bows.

31 Using felt-tipped pens, draw features on doll's face. Use lipstick on each side of the face for rosy cheeks.

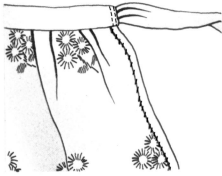

Johnny

Size
About $9\frac{1}{2}$in (24cm) tall.
A seam allowance of $\frac{1}{4}$in (5mm) has been included throughout.

Materials
One man's plain white cotton sock, size 9–11
Piece of blue/white gingham fabric $8\frac{1}{2}$×6in (21×15cm)
Piece of denim 14×6in (36×15cm)
Piece of yellow felt $5\frac{1}{2}$×2in (14×5cm)
$5\frac{1}{2}$in (14cm) square of red/white dotted cotton fabric
8in (20cm)-long $\frac{1}{8}$in (3mm)-thick green plant stick
Four $\frac{3}{8}$in (1cm)-diameter yellow buttons
Brown bouclé yarn; chenille needle
Piece of iron-on interfacing 5×$\frac{3}{4}$in (13×2cm)
Felt-tipped pens and lipstick
Tracing paper
Dressmaker's carbon
Suitable stuffing; pinking shears
Matching and contrasting sewing threads

16 Fold the dress in half, right sides together, at the shoulders. Pin, baste and stitch the side and underarm seams.

17 Make a double $\frac{1}{8}$in (3mm) hem at each wrist. Pin, baste and run a line of gathering stitches around each wrist hem.

18 Repeat step 17 around the neck edge.

24 Cut white tape in half. Tuck the ends of the tape into each end of the waistband. Pin, baste and stitch in place for apron strings. Tie apron around doll.

25 Fold one shoe top in half. Pin, baste and stitch back seam.

26 Match shoe sole to lower edge of shoe top. Blanket stitch the seam.

27 Repeat steps 25 and 26 to make other shoe in the same way.

28 Push feet into shoes, adding a little stuffing in the toes of the shoes. Sew shoes in place.

1 Make the boy's body as for the girl, steps 1 to 9.

2 Trace pattern pieces for the clothes given opposite.

3 Mark the pattern pieces on the wrong side of the appropriate fabrics the number of times stated. Cut out. Cut out shoe soles and tops from yellow felt.

4 Fold the shirt in half, right sides together, at the shoulders. Pin, baste and stitch side and underarm seams.

19 Make a double $\frac{1}{4}$in (5mm) hem around lower edge of dress. Pin, baste and stitch in place, using a zig-zag stitch.

20 Fit the dress over the doll. Pull up gathering stitches around neck and fasten off securely. Pull up gathering stitches around each wrist and fasten off securely.

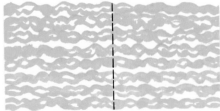

29 For the hair, cut out enough 9in (23cm) lengths of yarn to cover the head. Place yarn lengths together and stitch across the center to form a part.

21 Put the collar around the neck over dress with the collar ends meeting at front. Sew. Sew button at the neck.

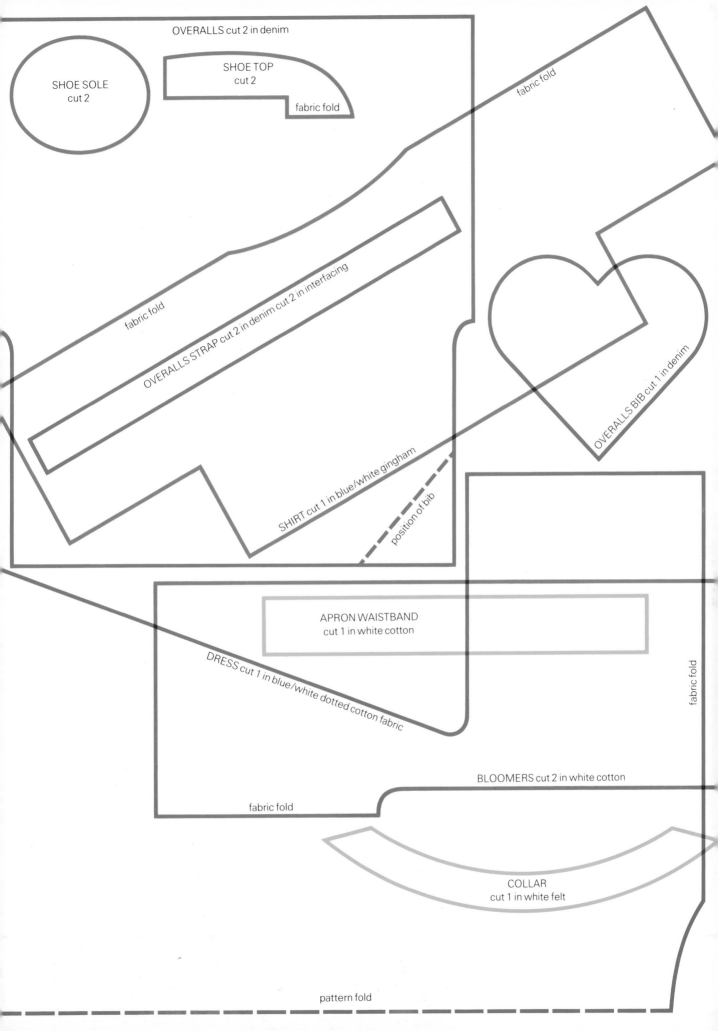

OVERALLS cut 2 in denim

SHOE SOLE
cut 2

SHOE TOP
cut 2

fabric fold

fabric fold

fabric fold

OVERALLS STRAP cut 2 in denim cut 2 in interfacing

OVERALLS BIB cut 1 in denim

SHIRT cut 1 in blue/white gingham

position of bib

APRON WAISTBAND
cut 1 in white cotton

fabric fold

DRESS cut 1 in blue/white dotted cotton fabric

BLOOMERS cut 2 in white cotton

fabric fold

COLLAR
cut 1 in white felt

pattern fold

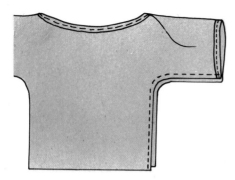

5 Make a ⅛in (3mm) double hem at neck edge. Pin, baste and run a line of gathering stitches around neck edge.
6 Make a ⅛in (3mm) double hem at the edge of each sleeve. Pin, baste and stitch in place.
7 Fit shirt over doll. Pull up gathering stitches around neck and fasten off securely.

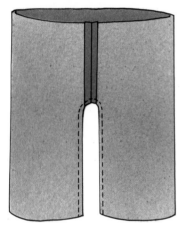

8 Place overall pieces together with right sides facing. Pin, baste and stitch back and front seams. Fold overalls with seams matching at the center. Pin, baste and stitch inner leg seams.
9 Make a ⅛in (3mm) double hem at top edge of overalls. Pin, baste and topstitch in place with two rows of stitching, using contrasting sewing thread.

10 Zig-zag stitch, using a contrasting sewing thread, all around the edge of the heart-shaped bib. Position bib over the top edge of the overalls, as marked on pattern. Pin, baste and stitch in place.

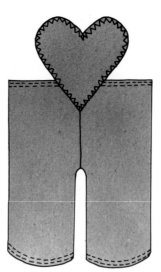

11 Make a double ⅛in (3mm) hem at the lower edge of each leg. Pin, baste and topstitch in place with two rows of stitching, using contrasting sewing thread.
12 Place interfacing on wrong side of each overall strap, with shiny side down. Iron in place. Topstitch lengthwise down the center of each strap using contrasting sewing thread.

13 Tuck one end of each strap under the top edge of the heart-shaped bib. Sew two buttons to bib where the straps meet to hold the straps in place. Fit the overalls on the doll. Take the straps over the shoulders, cross over at the back and fasten behind the overalls with two buttons as before.

14 Make shoes and fit them on the boy's feet as for the girl, steps 25 to 28.
15 For the hair use a single thickness of yarn and a sharp-pointed needle. Sew small loops all over the head, knotting the yarn at every stitch, so the hair will not come undone. When the head is covered, cut through all the loops. Trim if necessary.
16 Make features on boy's face, as for girl, step 31.

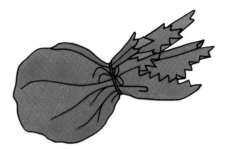

17 Use the dotted fabric for food bundle. Using pinking shears, pink around the edge of the fabric. Place some stuffing in the center of the fabric on the wrong side. Take up the four corners and bunch them together. Wind a length of matching sewing thread around the bunch and fasten off securely.

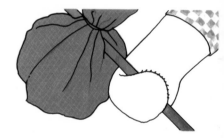

18 Cut a small hole through the bundle, just underneath the bound threads. Push the green stick through the hole. Sew the bundle firmly to one hand, turning the "fingers" around the stick.